art
YEAR BY YEAR

DK DELHI

Senior Art Editor Vikas Chauhan
Project Editor Neha Ruth Samuel
Project Art Editors Sanjay Chauhan, Heena Sharma
Editorial Team Shatarupa Chaudhuri, Upamanyu Das, Janashree Singha
Art Editor Sifat Fatima
Project Picture Researcher Aditya Katyal
Picture Research Manager Taiyaba Khatoon
Managing Editor Kingshuk Ghoshal
Managing Art Editor Govind Mittal
DTP Designers Ashok Kumar, Rakesh Kumar
Production Editor Anita Yadav
Pre-production Manager Balwant Singh
Production Manager Pankaj Sharma
Jacket Designer Juhi Sheth
Senior Jackets Coordinator Priyanka Sharma Saddi

DK LONDON

Senior Editor Pauline Savage
Senior Art Editor Sheila Collins
Senior US Editor Megan Douglass
US Executive Editor Lori Hand
Managing Editor Francesca Baines
Managing Art Editor Philip Letsu
Senior Production Controller Sian Cheung
Jacket Design Development Manager Sophia MTT
Publisher Andrew Macintyre
Associate Publishing Director Liz Wheeler
Art Director Karen Self
Publishing Director Jonathan Metcalf

First American Edition, 2022
Published in the United States by DK Publishing
1745 Broadway, 20th Floor, New York, NY 10019

Copyright © 2022 Dorling Kindersley Limited
DK, a Division of Penguin Random House LLC
22 23 24 25 26 10 9 8 7 6 5 4 3 2 1
001–314318–Nov/2022

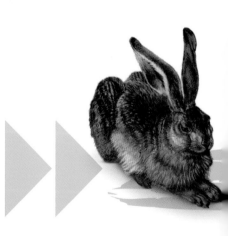

A catalog record for this book is available from the Library of Congress.
ISBN 978-0-7440-6012-6

DK books are available at special discounts when purchased in bulk for sales
DK Publishing Special Markets, 1745 Broadway, 20th Floor, New York, NY 10019
SpecialSales@dk.com

Printed and bound in China

For the curious
www.dk.com

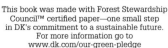

This book was made with Forest Stewardship
Council™ certified paper—one small step
in DK's commitment to a sustainable future.
For more information go to
www.dk.com/our-green-pledge

Smithsonian

Established in 1846, the Smithsonian is the world's largest museum
and research complex, dedicated to public education, national service,
and scholarship in the arts, sciences, and history. It includes 21
museums and galleries and the National Zoological Park. The total
number of artifacts, works of art, and specimens in the Smithsonian's
collection is estimated at 155.5 million.

S M I T H S O N I A N

art
YEAR BY YEAR

Written by
Alice Bowden, Peter Chrisp, Kate Devine,
Edward Dickenson, Bethan Durie,
Dr. Cynthia Fischer, and Justine Willis

Consultant
Dr. Cynthia Fischer

Contents

Traveling through time

The earliest art in this book was created a
long time ago. Some dates have BCE and CE after
them. These are short for "before the Common Era"
and "Common Era." The Common Era began with
the birth of Jesus. Where the exact date of an event
is not known, the letter "c" is used. This is short
for the Latin word *circa*, meaning "about," and
indicates that the date is approximate.

70,000 BCE–500 CE

From the earliest times, people have expressed themselves through simple designs on rocks and drawings on cave walls. Early humans created colors from earth and charcoal, and used them to paint vivid pictures of the animals they hunted. From c. 10,000 BCE, people settled in small communities and began making painted pots and vases. Around c. 3,000 BCE, the rise of the first great civilizations brought brilliantly detailed wall paintings and sculptures, and beautifully crafted objects, made to decorate palaces, temples, and tombs. These give a fascinating insight into the customs, religious beliefs, and artistic abilities of those who lived thousands of years ago.

c. 70,000 BCE

Original design

The world's oldest-known drawing—a pattern scratched on a lump of ocher rock—was found in the Blombos Cave in South Africa. The earliest art was purely decorative and did not show objects and creatures.

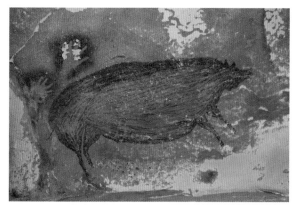

Life-size wall painting of a wild pig, Indonesia

c. 43,000 BCE

Wild art

This painting of a wild pig from a cave in Indonesia is the first known instance of art that shows something from the real world. Early people survived by hunting wild animals for food, and so these were the most common subject of early cave paintings.

— Crosshatch pattern

Engraved rock, South Africa

— The lion's ears are alert.

HAND STENCILS

Hand stencils are the most common form of cave art around the world, and may have been a signature—a way for people to leave their mark on places. They were made by pressing one hand against the cave wall and blowing a color pigment over and around it through a hollow bone or reed tube.

Cave of hands

Argentina's Cave of the Hands has hand stencils that have been made over thousands of years. Almost every available space in the cave is covered with them.

c. 38,000 BCE

The lion man

Found in the Hohlenstein-Stadel cave in southern Germany, this figure has the body of a man but the head and shoulders of a lion. It is the earliest work of art showing a being from the human imagination, rather than the real world. Made from the tusk of a mammoth, it took over 400 hours to carve, using only simple stone tools to shape the hard ivory.

Lion Man of Hohlenstein-Stadel, Germany

Black Venus of Dolni Vestonice, Czech Republic

The Black Venus is marked with the fingerprint of a child who held it thousands of years ago.

c. 14,000–12,000 BCE

Decorated weapons

Ice Age hunters turned their everyday objects into art. This spear-thrower, a device to make the spear fly faster, was found in France. Made from a reindeer antler, it was skillfully carved to resemble a mammoth.

c. 27,000–23,000 BCE

Ice Age Venus

People were always on the move during the Ice Age, and therefore made art that was easy to carry. Small Ice Age statues of the female body, nicknamed Venuses, have been found all across Europe. This Venus from the Czech Republic was formed of clay and ground-up bones, then baked in a fire.

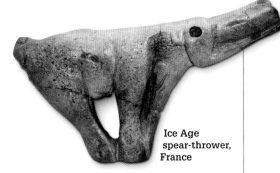

Ice Age spear-thrower, France

On the hunt

The Chauvet Cave in France is known for its animal paintings. The images were made by many different artists at different times. The overlapping images of these lions make it seem as if they are charging toward their prey.

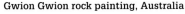

10,000 BCE

Gwion Gwion rock painting, Australia

c. 10,000 BCE

Rock painting

The First Nations artists of Australia painted scenes showing people, animals, and spirit beings on the walls of their rock shelters. The paintings usually depict stories of how the world was created. These slender figures with tassels and headdresses are known as Gwion Gwion, and are from the Kimberley region of Western Australia.

Natural pigments

Prehistoric artists made red, yellow, and brown pigments from crushed ocher (hematite). This was mixed with water or saliva, often in a shell, and painted onto walls using sticks, blowpipes, or fingers.

Prehistoric cave art

Rock art, such as paintings on the walls of caves, is the oldest art form in the world. In 1940, an underground cave full of paintings was discovered at Lascaux in southwestern France. Although it was named the Great Hall of the Bulls, the paintings in this cave also depict stags, bison, and horses—animals that were hunted regularly by the people who made these paintings. After the hunt, these people would rely only on their memory of the creatures to depict them. Since 1940, many other caves decorated with prehistoric animal paintings have been found. We can only guess why paintings were made inside dark caves, but it is likely that these sites were seen as special, powerful places.

Great Hall of the Bulls from the Lascaux cave

The Lascaux cave was **found by four boys** who were following their dog Robot, which had disappeared into a fox hole.

10,000 ▶ 3000 BCE

Wall painting of a
bull among people

Bulls were sacred to
the farming people
of Çatalhöyük.

c. 7300 BCE

Ancient wall art

Wall paintings were made in the world's earliest-known
town, Çatalhöyük in present-day Turkey. In this one, a crowd
surrounds a huge bull. The people have no weapons, so they
may be dancing or playing a game.

10,000 BCE

c. 9000 BCE

Life-size statue

This is the world's oldest life-
size sculpture of a human, from
Urfa in present-day Turkey. It
is made of sandstone and has
deep eye holes set with obsidian
(a black volcanic glass) and a
well-shaped nose. People in Urfa
began making large sculptures
after they had settled down
as a farming community.

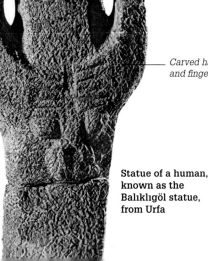

Carved hands
and fingers

Statue of a human,
known as the
Balıklıgöl statue,
from Urfa

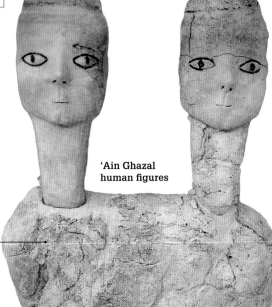

'Ain Ghazal
human figures

The bodies were
roughly shaped.

c. 6500 BCE

Recreating ancestors

At the settlement of 'Ain Ghazal in present-day Jordan, people
made half-life-size statues from bundles of reeds covered with
lime plaster. The statues may have represented their ancestors.
The sculptors carefully modeled the faces, while the lack of
limbs suggests that the statues may have been clothed.

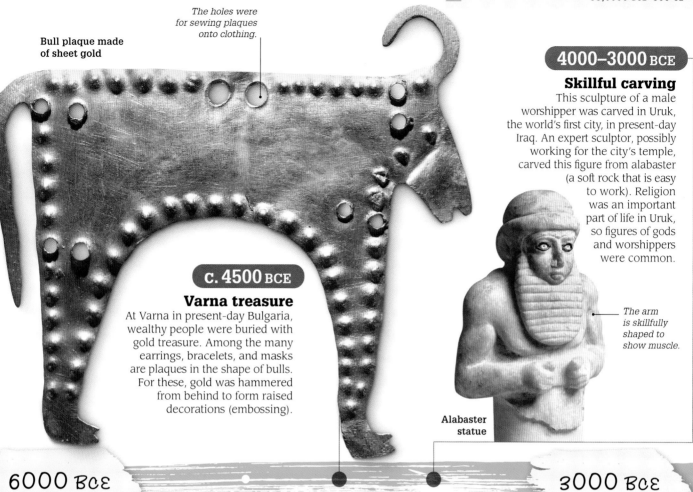

Bull plaque made of sheet gold

The holes were for sewing plaques onto clothing.

c. 4500 BCE
Varna treasure
At Varna in present-day Bulgaria, wealthy people were buried with gold treasure. Among the many earrings, bracelets, and masks are plaques in the shape of bulls. For these, gold was hammered from behind to form raised decorations (embossing).

4000–3000 BCE
Skillful carving
This sculpture of a male worshipper was carved in Uruk, the world's first city, in present-day Iraq. An expert sculptor, possibly working for the city's temple, carved this figure from alabaster (a soft rock that is easy to work). Religion was an important part of life in Uruk, so figures of gods and worshippers were common.

The arm is skillfully shaped to show muscle.

Alabaster statue

6000 BCE · · · 3000 BCE ▶▶

JADE CARVINGS

Jade is a precious stone that is usually green, but can be found in other colors, such as white and yellow. It is prized for its shine when polished and has been used by many cultures to make jewelery. The oldest jade carvings date from c. 4000–3000 BCE, and were made by the Hongshan people of northeast China. They carved amulets as burial offerings. In Chinese culture, jade came to represent immortality, possibly due to its hardness and durability.

The bird has a sharp beak.

Owl amulet
From the Hongshan culture, this green jade amulet (protective charm) is in the form of a bird, probably an owl, with big eyes and talons. Its form has been simplified, or stylized, to make a striking design.

Jomon pottery
Hunter-gatherers in Japan made the first clay pots in c. 14,500 BCE, which they decorated to look like woven baskets. These cooking vessels are known as "Jomon" (cord-patterned) pots, and were artistic as well as practical.

The raised cord patterns were made by attaching rolled pieces of clay.

Jomon pot

13

3000 ▸ 1550 BCE

c. 2800–2700 BCE
Cycladic harpist
In Greece's Cyclades islands, sculptors carved small marble statuettes of men and women with simplified, often flat, faces. This sitting male figure is a musician plucking the strings of a harp with his thumb. Cycladic sculptures, which appear white, were originally painted, although almost nothing remains of the colors.

The slightly raised head suggests that the musician may be singing.

Traces of paint

Statue of harp player in marble

Copper head of an Akkadian ruler

c. 2300 BCE
Regal head
A head made of copper is all that remains of a life-size statue of a king of Akkad in Mesopotamia (modern-day Iraq). It would have had eyes inlaid with jewels, later stolen by the king's enemies. The elaborately braided hair and distinctive headband show his high status.

3000 BCE

1550 BCE

Standard of Ur

People are eating and drinking at the banquet.

The figure is 4 in (11 cm) tall.

Dancing Girl

c. 2500 BCE
Bronze dancer
An early example of a bronze sculpture is this figurine of a woman from Mohenjo Daro in modern-day Pakistan. She is wearing bangles and other jewelery, and her legs are bent, suggesting that she may be dancing.

c. 2500 BCE
Mesopotamian mosaic
Found in a royal tomb in Ur, Mesopotamia (modern-day Iraq), this ancient box is decorated with mosaics of shells, lapis lazuli, and sandstone. This side of the box shows a procession of animals, with a royal feast at the top.

c. 3000–30 BCE   EGYPTIAN ART

The homes of some ancient Egyptian people were filled with decorative objects. These items were also placed in tombs, where they served a specific purpose beyond decoration: to help people in the afterlife. Tombs contained paintings of the dead leading a happy life, and mummified people were buried with treasures, which the Egyptians believed could be carried to the afterlife. This beautifully made art gives an insight into the beliefs of this civilization.

Hieroglyphs are words in the form of pictures.

Nebamun's wife Hatshepsut watches over him.

Golden burial mask
The pharaoh (ruler) Tutankhamen, who died as a teenager, was buried wearing a solid gold mask. Weighing more than 22 lb (10 kg), it was inlaid with colored glass and semiprecious stones. The mask was made to serve as the pharaoh's perfect new face in the afterlife.

Hunting in the afterlife
In paintings of the human body, the upper body was depicted from the front, while all other parts of the body were shown side on. In this painting from a tomb, a scribe (official) called Nebamun hunts birds in the marshes of the Nile River with his family.

Glass fish
This decorative fish, found in a person's house, is actually a glass bottle for ointments or cosmetics. It was made by wrapping heated rods of colored glass around a mud model of a fish, and then dragging a needle over the surface to create a pattern resembling fish scales.

Life after death
Much of what we know about ancient Egypt is from the detailed, painted wooden models of scenes from daily life found in tombs. Boats, such as this Nile River vessel, were believed to provide the dead with transportation in the afterlife.

A lookout standing in the bow of the boat scans for dangers on the river.

Animals in art

People have depicted animals in their works of art from the earliest times. Working animals, such as camels, elephants, and horses, appear in the art of many cultures, showing the valuable role they play in everyday life. While some artists capture an animal's likeness accurately, others take a more imaginative approach, making them into fantastical creatures or playful objects. More recently, a new theme has emerged: the story of wildlife under threat.

Wild paradise, c. 200 BCE

A Roman mosaic from Pompeii, Italy, depicts the animals and plants native to the Nile River in Egypt, including date palms, a snarling hippopotamus, a snappy crocodile, and two sacred ibises. Tiny pieces of stone were pieced together very precisely to create the textures, colors, and patterns of the animals' feathers, fur, and scales. The artist has even managed to portray their characters.

The rider is larger than his horse, suggesting his importance. The statues were usually around 27½ in (70 cm) tall.

Decorative headdress

Cylindrical legs

Terra-cotta horseman, c. 1200–1500

Medieval West African kingdoms had cavalry (horseback warriors), and terra-cotta sculptures found in Africa's Mopti region (in present-day Mali) include riders on horseback. This one was made in the Djenné art style, named after an ancient town in Mopti. The elaborate headgear worn by the horse and its rider, and their tube-shaped bodies and legs, are typical of this style. Horses may have represented wealth and power to the people of this region.

The camel's head is made up of animal and human faces.

Animal of many faces, c. 1500

A close look at this painting from Persia (present-day Iran) reveals that the camel is formed from all sorts of interlocking figures, from rabbits to demons. The style became popular in the 16th century and may have represented a spiritual belief of Sufism (a branch of Islamic faith), that all creatures exist together within God.

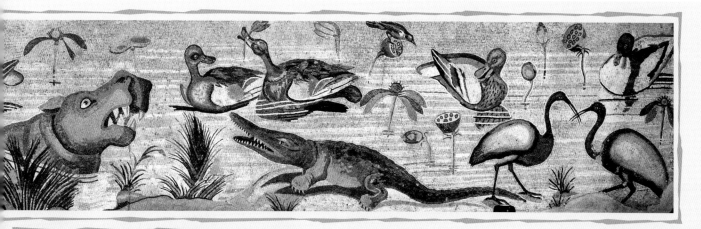

Princely elephant, c. 1500–1600

Khem Karan, a well-known artist from India's Mughal era, painted this miniature in rich colors. Elephants were valuable to the Indian imperial court at the time, and court artists were often asked to produce portraits of favorite animals. The gold rings and bells on the elephant hint at its owner's high status.

The smooth surface is comfortable to hold.

A curious rabbit, c. 1800

A *netsuke* is a traditional Japanese fastening, around 1–3in (2.5–7.5cm) in size, used with a cord to hang a pouch from a sash. Many are carefully carved to look like animals. The size and shape of this ivory rabbit make it perfect for the job because it is light and rounded.

Recycled ocean predator, 2016

From luminous seaweed to the shark's spiky jaws, this entire sculpture was created from plastic waste collected from the sea or beach as part of a community project in the United States. The project celebrates ocean life, draws attention to problems caused by plastic garbage, and encourages conservation of marine animals.

Caught in the act, 1891

Is this tiger surprised or is it surprising its prey? Who can tell! In his painting *Surprised!*, self-taught French painter Henri Rousseau used bold shapes, rich colors, and diagonal brushstrokes to conjure up a stormy jungle in the naive (simple and informal) style—without ever leaving his native country or seeing a real jungle.

1550 ▶ 500 BCE

c. 1450–1400 BCE

Colorful fresco

The Minoans were a civilization from Crete. Bulls feature heavily in their art, and may have been considered sacred. This wall painting from the palace of Knossos, on Crete, shows young Minoans leaping over a huge bull in what was perhaps a ritual.

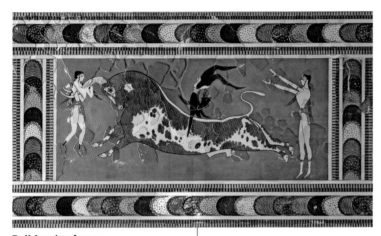

Bull-leaping fresco

RECONSTRUCTING FRESCOES

Minoan paintings were made while the wall plaster was still wet—a method later called "fresco" ("fresh" in Italian). The plaster absorbed the colors, keeping the paintings from fading. Many Minoan paintings have survived only as tiny pieces of painted plaster.

The blue background is mostly modern.

Jigsaw pieces

In 1901–1902, Swiss artist Émile Victor Guilliéron reconstructed the bull fresco using plaster fragments found on the floor of the palace of Knossos. The process was like putting together a jigsaw puzzle with many pieces missing.

1550 ● ● ○ **1000**

---

c. 1600–1046 BCE

Bronze mask

The Sanxingdui culture of Shang Dynasty China made monumental bronze sculptures, some as tall as 13 ft (4 m). The faces of the human sculptures typically had exaggerated features, such as this one with fanned-out ears, a beaklike nose, and eyes that stick out as if on stalks.

The queen wears a flat-topped crown with a decorative ribbon.

c. 1340 BCE

A queen's likeness

This ancient Egyptian painted limestone bust of Queen Nefertiti is one of the world's most famous sculptures. It was created by Thutmose, Pharaoh Akhenaten's chief sculptor. He made it as a model for other sculptors to follow when making statues of the beautiful queen.

The green color is verdigris, which occurs when bronze is exposed to the weather.

Bust of Nefertiti

Sanxingdui bronze mask

Giant Olmec head

The headgear may be a helmet, worn when playing a ball game or in battle.

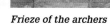

Frieze of the archers

c. 900 BCE

Basalt bust

The Olmec people lived in the region that is now part of modern-day Mexico. They were expert carvers who created massive stone heads—the largest is 11 ft (3.4 m) high. Crafted from basalt, a hard volcanic stone, these are individual portraits, probably of rulers.

c. 510 BCE

Persian soldiers

This colorful, decorated wall, made using glazed bricks, was found among the ruins of a palace in Susa, Iran. It shows the "Immortals"— the royal guards of the Persian king Darius I. The soldiers are identical apart from the hand-painted patterns on their long robes.

500 ▶▶

c. 900–700 BCE

Phoenician ivory

The Phoenicians lived in the area that is now Lebanon. Phoenician artists were influenced by the art of the cultures they traded with, such as Egypt and Mesopotamia. This ivory carving depicts the mythical Sphinx from Egypt, but with wings—a feature of Mesopotamian sphinxes.

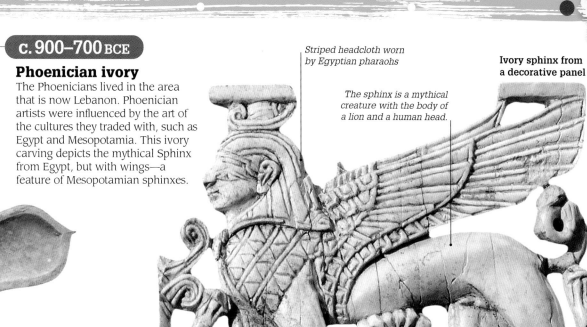

Striped headcloth worn by Egyptian pharaohs

The sphinx is a mythical creature with the body of a lion and a human head.

Ivory sphinx from a decorative panel

Fanlike shapes, resembling lotus flowers

The Phoenicians were skilled glass-makers. They exported their items all around the Mediterranean.

A journey through the underworld

Book of the Dead, c. 1275 BCE, Unknown artist

Egyptian art was often based on a belief in the afterlife—life after death. First, the dead would have to travel through the dangerous underworld, where the gods would decide whether they were worthy of the afterlife. To help them on their journey, a dead person would be buried with a collection of magic spells called a *Book of the Dead*. This one, painted on papyrus, is for a scribe (official) called Hunefer. Read from left to right, this scene shows a ceremony called the Weighing of the Heart.

Protecting Hunefer

The jackal-headed god Anubis protects Hunefer on his journey. Anubis leads Hunefer by the hand to a set of scales, where the god will weigh his heart against the feather of truth.

Ammut, the devourer

The weighing determines if a person has been dishonest in life, which would make their heart heavier than the feather. If it is, the heart is eaten by Ammut, a goddess who is part crocodile, lion, and hippopotamus.

Ra, the sun god

Hunefer worships Ra, the sun god and the creator of all things, who has a solar disk on his head. Ra is one of 14 gods at the top of the painting, who will all help Hunefer on his journey.

Isis and Nephthys

Standing behind Osiris are his sisters—Isis, the goddess of healing (left), and Nephthys, the protector of the dead. Their names are shown by hieroglyphs above their heads. Isis's sign is a throne, while her sister's symbol is a basket on top of a house.

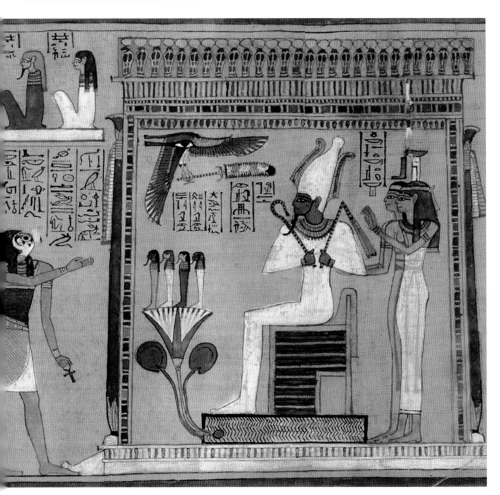

Osiris, the king

Osiris's kingship is shown by his tall crown and the crook and flail in his hands. Although he wears the white wrappings of the dead, his green skin, the color of vegetation, represents new life. Seated on his throne, Osiris welcomes Hunefer into the kingdom of the dead.

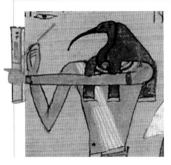

Thoth, the scribe

Thoth, the god of wisdom and writing, has the head of an ibis bird. He records on a clay tablet that Hunefer's heart has been found to be truthful and just. The same judgment is recorded in the hieroglyphs (writing in the form of symbols) on the papyrus.

Horus, the sky god

Hunefer is taken on the last part of his journey by Horus, the falcon-headed sky god. Horus leads the scribe to the throne of his father Osiris, king of the underworld. He tells Osiris that Hunefer is worthy of entering his kingdom.

500 ▶ 100 BCE

The sculptures usually have raised eyebrows.

The mane is made with orange-brown pebbles.

Darker pebbles show the lion's muscles.

Lion Hunt mosaic

c. 500–200 BCE

Terra-cotta figures

The earliest African art south of the Sahara are the Nok terra-cottas—pottery sculptures of animals and human heads that are named after the village in Nigeria where they were first found. The human sculptures have a variety of hairstyles and headwear, but most share the same open mouths and triangular eyes.

Nok terra-cotta head

Late 300s BCE

Pebble mosaics

The Greeks were highly skilled in the art of mosaic, using thousands of different-colored uncut pebbles or tiny tiles to make floor decorations. This lion mosaic is a masterpiece of the early pebble technique. It was made in Pella, the birthplace of Alexander the Great and capital of Macedonia (in modern-day Greece).

▶▶ 500 BCE

Etruscan tomb painting

c. 375 BCE

Mysterious lady

The Lady of Elche is a limestone bust from Spain made by an ancient Iberian civilization, representing either a goddess or a real person. Her high status is evident from her jewelery and elaborate headdress with wheel-like coils at the sides. Her expression is difficult to decipher, but the gaze of her eyes is hard to avoid.

Following the customs of Greek vase painting, the woman is shown with lighter skin than the man.

c. 470 BCE

Tomb dancers

The Etruscans, from northwest and central Italy, were highly skilled artists and created realistic depictions of their world. This wall painting is of a male and female dancer. Although it decorates a tomb, it shows a joyful celebration of life.

The Lady of Elche

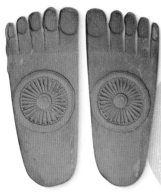

Symbolic Buddha

The founder of Buddhism, Gautama Buddha, was first represented by symbols rather than shown in human form. These pottery feet from India symbolize his footprints, and the wheel of law at their center represents his teachings.

C. 210 BCE

Ancient soldier

This sculpture of a warrior belongs to an army of more than 7,000 life-size terra-cotta figures, buried with the first emperor of China to protect him in the afterlife. Each sculpture is detailed and unique. The uniform and hairstyle show each warrior's rank in the army.

This soldier has a topknot tied with cloth wrappings.

Kneeling archer from the Terra-Cotta Army

100 BCE

The armor was once decorated with bright colors.

The hands would have held a crossbow.

C. 500–300 BCE   GREEK ART

During the Classical Age (c. 500 BCE–323 BCE), Greek art and architecture was at its peak. Sculptors and painters depicted Greek myths, showing gods and heroes with perfectly proportioned bodies. Greek artwork, such as painted vases and stone statues, were widely admired around the Mediterranean world.

A scene from a Greek myth depicting the goddess Athena

Two warriors fight before the gods Hermes and Athena.

Vase with black figures

On the early vases, figures such as these warriors were painted in black, with lines for muscles carved into the surface.

Vase with red figures

With the later styles the background was painted black and the figures left in the red of the clay. Details were painted with a brush.

New carving style

The Greeks were experts at relief carving, in which figures stand out from a flat base. This lifelike marble relief by the famous sculptor Phidias is from the Parthenon temple in Athens, and shows worshippers in a procession.

Shipwreck survivor

This statue, found in a shipwreck, is a rare example of a surviving Greek bronze. It is thought to represent Zeus, the king of the gods, though it has also been suggested that it might be his brother Poseidon, god of the sea.

The position of the arm suggests he was holding a thunderbolt, Zeus's weapon.

Hollow cast bronze statue of Zeus or Poseidon

Mosaic battle scene

Alexander Mosaic, c. 100 BCE, Unknown artist

Nearly 1.5 million small tiles make up this mosaic from the ancient Roman city of Pompeii in Italy. It is a copy of a lost Greek painting from the 3rd century BCE. The mosaic depicts the victory of Alexander the Great of Macedonia over King Darius of Persia in battle, sometime between 331 BCE and 333 BCE. The dramatic scene shows the two mighty leaders staring at each other above the chaos and confusion of the battlefield.

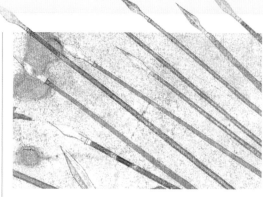

A forest of spikes
These long spears, called *sarissas*, were used by Macedonian cavalry and foot soldiers. They show that the scene is part of a bigger battle and make it feel like the Persians are hemmed in by the advancing Greek army.

Alexander's grim stare
The mosaic depicts Alexander as a heroic figure, leading a cavalry charge, with his eyes fixed on Darius. Riding on his horse Bucephalus, Alexander spears a Persian horseman without even looking at him.

Sad reflection
A dying Persian soldier, fallen beneath a fleeing horse, sees his own reflection in a shield. The artist skillfully shows light and shadow on the shield, as well as the suffering on the soldier's face.

Darius in terror

The Persian king looks back at Alexander with terror in his eyes, his right arm outstretched in a helpless gesture. Though he has a bow in his left hand, he does not even try to use it as he flees the battlefield.

Trying to escape

Desperate to escape from the battlefield and save his king from the approaching Alexander, the Persian charioteer furiously whips the horses. Like all the Persian soldiers in the scene, he wears a light brown hood.

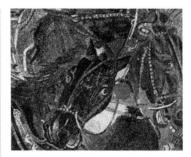

Panicked horses

In the middle of all the chaos, the chariot horses panic. They pull in different directions, with their heads at all angles. They have wild eyes and open mouths with bared teeth.

c. 100–1 BCE

Ornate drinking cup

A rhyton is a horn-shaped luxury vessel that was used by ancient peoples to pour or drink wine. This rhyton was made from gilded silver by the Parthians (who lived in present-day Iran). At the spout's end we see the front of a lion, whose eyes are set with a red gemstone called garnet.

Gilded silver rhyton

Small hole for spout

The woman's gold jewelery shows she was wealthy.

Egyptian mummy portrait

c. 1–300 CE

Painting the dead

During the period of Roman rule in Egypt, Greek artists painted portraits of the dead to decorate mummy cases. Unlike earlier Egyptian mummy portraits, they were realistic portrayals of individual people, like this one of an upper-class woman.

100 BCE

50 CE

27 BCE–476 CE   ROMAN ART

Many of the artists working across the Roman Empire were Greeks. The Romans so admired famous Greek works of art that they often asked Greek artists to make copies of them. Public places, such as bathhouses, and the homes of the wealthy were filled with sculptures, wall paintings, and mosaics. The Romans were also master glassmakers, using new methods such as glass-blowing.

Largest cameo

The *Great Cameo of France*, made in the 1st century CE, is the largest surviving ancient Roman cameo—a carving from stone with colored layers. The five layers of sardonyx (a multicolored stone) were carved to create a relief where the Roman imperial family look like Greek gods.

This cameo is 12 in (31 cm) high and 10⅓ in (26.5 cm) wide.

Godly emperor

The first Roman emperor, Augustus, always wanted his statues to make him look like a handsome young man, even though he lived to be 75. In this 1st-century-CE marble sculpture, his raised hand shows he is addressing his troops, while the bare feet and Cupid link him to the gods.

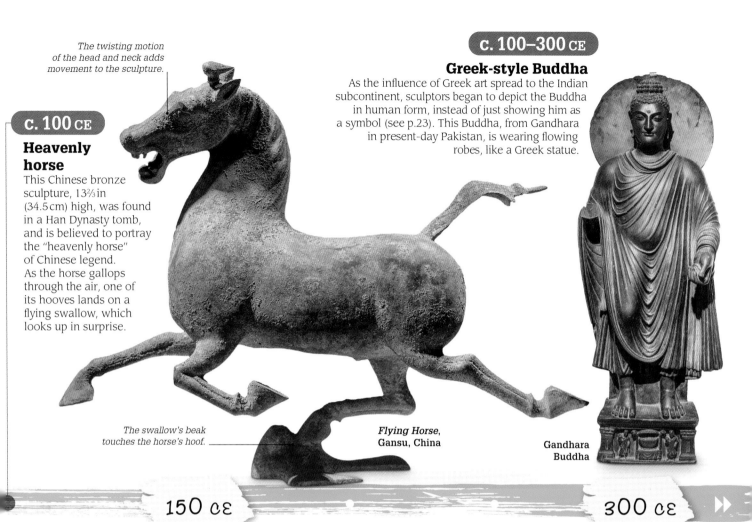

The twisting motion of the head and neck adds movement to the sculpture.

c. 100 CE

Heavenly horse

This Chinese bronze sculpture, 13⅔in (34.5cm) high, was found in a Han Dynasty tomb, and is believed to portray the "heavenly horse" of Chinese legend. As the horse gallops through the air, one of its hooves lands on a flying swallow, which looks up in surprise.

The swallow's beak touches the horse's hoof.

Flying Horse, Gansu, China

c. 100–300 CE

Greek-style Buddha

As the influence of Greek art spread to the Indian subcontinent, sculptors began to depict the Buddha in human form, instead of just showing him as a symbol (see p.23). This Buddha, from Gandhara in present-day Pakistan, is wearing flowing robes, like a Greek statue.

Gandhara Buddha

150 CE

300 CE

Garden in a garden

This fresco of a Roman garden, dating back to the 1st century CE, was found in the home of a wealthy family in Pompeii, Italy. It decorated the wall of an outdoor dining room that faced a garden, and the painting features stunning details of birds and flowers.

Colorful glassware

Glass-blowing allowed vessels, such as this beautiful vase, to be produced in large numbers. The hand-painted decoration on this piece, which dates back to the 1st century CE, depicts the Greek myth of Europa, riding Zeus (Jupiter) in the form of a bull. The loose brush strokes suggest it was painted quickly.

*Mosaic of the
Female Musicians*

**Spout for
pouring liquid**

**Boys dressed
as cupids work
the foot pump,
which delivers
air to the pipes
in the organ.**

c. 300–600

Portrait pottery

The Moche people of northern Peru were skilled potters. They made vessels that were lifelike portraits of individual people, which was unique among Indigenous art from the Americas. All surviving portrait pots show men, most probably Moche rulers.

c. 350–399

Musical mosaic

This striking Byzantine mosaic from Syria shows a group of six richly dressed female musicians and two boys, performing in a theater. Their instruments include a set of bowls and a pipe organ. The wonderful details of the mosaic—the shadows, the knots in the wooden planks of the floor, and the intricate decorations on the instruments—show that it was created by a highly skilled artist.

300

**The headband
is painted in
geometric
patterns.**

c. 350–399

Depicting Christ

After Christianity became an official Roman religion, Roman artists began to make images of Christ. Most of these initial images depicted him clean shaven, like a Roman emperor. This wall painting from Rome is one of the first to show Christ with a beard and long hair—a look that is similar to depictions of the Roman god Jupiter.

**Moche
portrait pot**

 Moche portrait pots are so realistic
that they show faces with wrinkles,
scars, and twisted mouths.

**Bearded Christ mural from the
catacomb of Commodilla, Italy**

320–554 CE   GUPTA ART

The Gupta Dynasty ruled over most of northern India from 320–554 CE. Under its leadership, the arts developed and thrived. The Guptas were Hindus, and revived some ancient Hindu artistic traditions. They created a new style of temple that was freestanding, and made of stone or brick rather than wood, which had been used previously. Buddhist art also flourished, and Buddhist cave shrines and temples of the period are decorated with some of the finest paintings to survive from ancient India.

Buddhist cave paintings

This portrait of *bodhisattva* Padmapani, who represents compassion, is perhaps the best known of the Buddhist paintings from the cave shrines of Ajanta (in present-day Maharashtra, India). His down-turned eyes show care for others, while the crown on his head indicates his divine status.

Hindu sculptures

The walls of many Gupta-era temples are decorated with striking terra-cotta sculptures depicting scenes from Hindu mythology. This one shows Krishna, a human form of the Hindu God Vishnu, defeating and killing a horse-demon called Keshi.

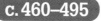

400

500

Colossus of Barletta

Jeweled diadem

Globe shows his claim to rule the world

c. 460–495

Buddha in rock

As Buddhism spread from India to China, many artists in China took inspiration from Indian art styles, such as copying the Gupta tradition of carving cave shrines and large Buddhas out of rock. Part of a temple complex in Yungang, China, this 45-ft (14-m) Buddha statue also reflects Gupta influence in the Buddha's calm expression and the clothes worn by the figures.

c. 400–450

Bronze leader

Almost three times life size, this bronze statue shows a Byzantine emperor, who has not been identified. Its armor and pose, with a raised right arm, are inspired by statues of the Roman emperor, Augustus (see p.26). The statue was made in Constantinople (present-day Istanbul, Turkey), and now stands in Barletta, Italy. The cross in the figure's right hand was added in 1431, replacing a lost spear.

Buddha with attendant at Yungang, Northeast China

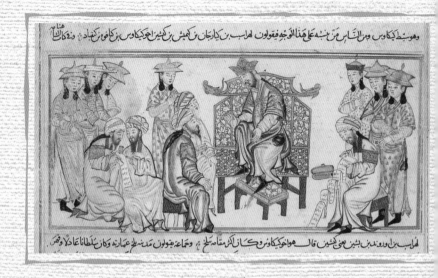

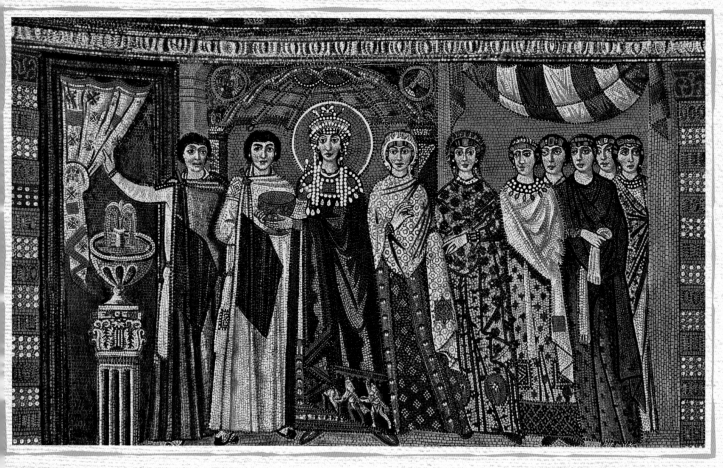

500–1400

As old empires ended and new ones were created, people found unique ways to express how they saw themselves and their changing world. Vast cities in Mesoamerica were bustling with creativity, producing gold ornaments, pottery, and stone carvings. The Byzantine Empire of Europe became known for its lavish mosaics and gilded Christian icons. The spread of Buddhism in Asia brought new ways of celebrating life and commemorating death in art. In Africa, highly skilled artists created lifelike busts and elaborate sculptures from bronze and ivory. Islamic artists developed designs based on geometric shapes, natural patterns, and calligraphy rather than the human form.

Persian silver and gold plate

Mural from Prince Xu Xianxiu's tomb

c. 500

Mysterious heads

When seven terra-cotta heads were discovered in Mashishing, South Africa, between 1957 and 1966, they were among some of the oldest artifacts found in southern Africa. Although not identical, they have similar features. Their original use remains a mystery. This one, however, may have been a mask that could be slipped on like a helmet.

Mashishing head

An animal, possibly a lion, perches on top.

Neck rings may represent prosperity and beauty.

c. 571

Inside a tomb

Magnificent large murals adorn the tomb of Prince Xu Xianxiu of China's Northern Qi Dynasty. Considered among this era's finest art, they show the grandeur of this dynasty. One of them depicts Xu and his wife at a feast, surrounded by musicians. Lotus blossoms above them show that Xu was a Buddhist.

c. 500

Precious plate

During the rule of the Sasanian Dynasty in Persia, artisans crafted silver plates with reliefs on them, which were given as royal gifts, mainly to rulers of other kingdoms. This gilded plate depicts a Sasanian king hunting rams, a sport which displayed his skill and strength.

500

550

Empress Theodora wears a crown set with pearls and gems.

An imperial canopy covers the group.

c. 527–547

Celebrated mosaics

The Church of San Vitale in Ravenna, Italy, contains some of the most striking and colorful examples of Byzantine mosaics. They include this one of Theodora, Byzantine empress of the Eastern Roman Empire, and her attendants. The expensive fabrics and the fountain in the scene show she is a person of high status.

Mosaic from the Church of San Vitale

The speech bubble with seashells and plants represents a prayer for water.

Mural of a
Teotihuacan rain priest

The priest wears a decorative headdress.

c. 500–600

Rain ceremony

The ancient city of Teotihuacan, near modern-day Mexico City, was known for its architecture and elaborately decorated temples and homes. This mural fragment was part of a larger fresco painted on the walls of a palace. It shows a rain priest performing a ceremony that took place every 52 years.

600

650

Haniwa warrior

c. 500–600

Hollow figures

During the Kofun Period in Japan, hollow clay sculptures called *haniwa* were arranged in circles on top of enormous, mound-shaped tombs. These sculptures were made in various forms, from people to animals, and even buildings. Many of them were figures of warriors, wielding swords, bows, and quivers of arrows.

The Sutton Hoo helmet

c. 580–620

Anglo-Saxon find

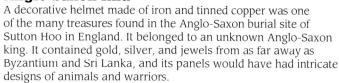

A decorative helmet made of iron and tinned copper was one of the many treasures found in the Anglo-Saxon burial site of Sutton Hoo in England. It belonged to an unknown Anglo-Saxon king. It contained gold, silver, and jewels from as far away as Byzantium and Sri Lanka, and its panels would have had intricate designs of animals and warriors.

33

728
Tomb treasures
At this time in China, decorative objects were made to be buried with the dead, for use in the afterlife. *Sancai* ("three-color") earthenware figures and pottery, such as this camel, were popular tomb figures, and showed that its owner was wealthy.

Demon mask to ward off evil

Splashes of green, amber, and white paint are used to glaze this figurine.

Sancai camel figure

c. 600–999 CE
Blow the whistle
This clay figure from Nopiloa in modern-day Mexico is actually a whistle, probably for use in religious rituals. It is modeled as a ballplayer—ball games were an important part of Mesoamerican culture. The figure is decorated with symbols commonly used in Maya art at the time. For instance, a knotted rope, such as the one around his neck and wrist, indicated a captured prisoner.

650

700

The ballplayer wears large, cylindrical ear ornaments.

c. 707
Painted instructions
A wall painting from an ancient cathedral in Faras, in modern-day Sudan, shows Saint Anne, the mother of Mary and grandmother of Jesus. The saint holds a finger to her lips, making a gesture of silence. The painting may have encouraged worshippers to pray silently.

A bulky waistband shielded the player from the ball.

Mesoamerican ballplayer

Fragment of wall painting depicting Saint Anne

 Mesoamerican ball games were not always friendly matches, and sometimes ended in violence or even death!

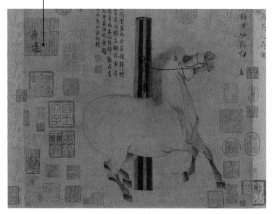

The red stamps are from the picture's various owners, all showing off that they own it.

Night-Shining White

c. 750
A spirited beast
Horses, which represented wealth and power, were a popular subject in Chinese art. The horse seems to be in a fiery mood, with glaring eyes and flaring nostrils, in this ink painting called *Night-Shining White* by Han Gan, a leading artist of the Tang Dynasty.

ILLUMINATED MANUSCRIPTS

Before the invention of the printing press, books were copied painstakingly by hand, some taking years of work. In Europe and the Arab world, most important books, including religious ones, would be illustrated with beautiful patterns and figures, often decorated with real gold and gemstones.

Large letters filled with knot and spiral patterns began each of the Gospels.

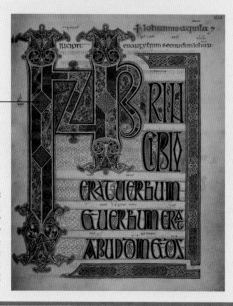

The Lindisfarne Gospels
Made in the 8th century by monks in Anglo-Saxon England, this intricately patterned manuscript contains four books—called the Gospels—from the Bible. As well as Celtic patterns, the manuscript also contains Germanic and Mediterranean styles, showing how far influences traveled.

750 — ● — ● — 800 ▶▶

c. 770–800
Cultural mix
The ancient Scots, known as the Picts by the Romans, carved this stone slab in the small Scottish village of Aberlemno. This side shows a battle scene with Celtic symbols above it, and on the back is a large cross. While the use of this stone slab is unknown, it highlights how Celtic and Christian cultures mingled at this time.

Daibutsu in Todai-ji Temple, Nara, Japan

Pictish stone carving

752
Colossal Buddha
After Japan embraced Buddhism as an official religion in the 6th century, statues of the Buddha were widely created by artists and craftspeople. This colossal bronze statue of the Buddha is the largest of its kind in the world. Called a *daibutsu*, meaning "giant Buddha," the statue is 49 ft (15 m) tall and weighs nearly 550 tons (500 metric tons).

Maya rituals
Yaxchilán Lintel 24, c. 723–726, Unknown artist

Yaxchilán was an important ancient Maya city in the region that is modern-day Mexico. It is known for its elaborate stone carvings, such as this limestone lintel (a support placed above a door or window). These carvings depict the history and religious rituals of the Maya, giving a fascinating insight into their culture as well as their art. This example is from a grand building, and shows Maya ruler Itzamnaaj B'ahlam II and his wife, Lady K'ab'al Xook, who is performing a ritual.

Ceremonial torch
The king holds a flaming torch, described in the glyphs as a "burning spear," over his wife. This indicates that the ritual may be taking place at night, or inside a dark chamber.

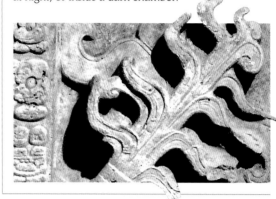

An important leader
Itzamnaaj B'ahlam II ruled over a period of great artistic and political development in Yaxchilán, during which he oversaw the creation of a number of temples and monuments. He wears a headdress with a shrunken head attached to the front—possibly a battle trophy.

Royal jewelery
Lady Xook was a powerful royal figure. Here she is wearing elaborate jewelery, which was probably made from jade, a green stone of great value in Maya society. Her pectoral (chest badge) is a representation of the Maya sun god.

Faded pigments
The lintels were originally painted using natural dyes. The Maya favored shades of blue and green over other colors. Although the paint has worn off over time, traces of blue, turquoise, and red pigments remain on the stone sculpture.

A moment in time
The top and left edges of the lintel feature Maya glyphs, a pictorial language. They include important details about what is happening in the scene. These two glyphs tell us the exact date of the ritual: October 24, 709 CE.

Bloodletting ritual
Lady Xook runs a rope studded with sharp obsidian (a volcanic rock) through her tongue, spilling blood. The ritual of bloodletting originated from a Maya creation story that told of how the gods spilled blood to create humans.

**Wood carving
of an animal head**

Ancient icon

This image, consisting of
21 painted ceramic tiles,
is a depiction of St. Theodore
Stratelates, a revered saint who is
often shown as a warrior. It was
found in the ruins of the Patleina
Monastery, near Preslav in
Bulgaria. It is the country's
oldest surviving icon.

**Icon of St. Theodore
Stratelates**

c. 820

Viking carvings

This fearsome-looking animal
head is one of five found in a buried
Viking ship in Oseberg, Norway.
Standing at 20 in (50 cm) high,
it was carved from a single tree
trunk that had a natural curve.
The intricate details suggest it
was crafted by an expert. Its
purpose remains a mystery.

Viking kings and
other important people
were often buried in
their boats, perhaps
to help them travel
to the afterlife.

800

850

**Stone relief from
Borobudur Temple**

c. 800

Temple relief

Borobudur Temple in Java, Indonesia,
was built over the course of the 8th and
9th centuries. Its walls are decorated
with 160 carved relief panels. This
panel shows the law of *karma*—the
belief that all actions have consequences.
The figures on the right have been
cooking turtles and fish, forbidden
foods for Buddhists, so in the middle
of the panel, they are boiled in a
big pot themselves.

Buddhist
masterpiece

Borobudur is the world's
largest Buddhist temple
complex, with 72 statues of
the Buddha, each placed inside
a stupa. Its multiple levels
represent the stages followers
must travel through to
reach enlightenment.

c. 800–900

Hindu sculpture

God Vishnu, one of the three main deities of Hinduism, is the subject of this brass and silver sculpture from northern India. At Vishnu's side are two figures who represent his weapons—on the left stands Gadadevi, holding his *gada* (mace), and on the right stands Chakra Purusha with his *chakra* (discus).

Vishnu's four arms represent his roles in both the physical and spiritual worlds.

Figure of God Vishnu

900

c. 871–899

Made for a king

This tear-shaped object, whose purpose is unknown, has an inscription that says, "Alfred ordered me to be made." This shows that it belonged to Alfred the Great, the king of the Saxon kingdom of Wessex in southwestern England. Made from gold and rock crystal, it was found in the marshlands where Alfred famously hid while planning a counterattack during a battle.

The Alfred Jewel

Igbo ornament

This little 9th-century bronze pendant, in the form of a human head, is from Igbo-Ukwu, Nigeria. The pattern of scars on the cheeks and forehead were associated with Igbo men of high status, so it may have been made for an important person.

ART IN MANY FORMS

Many of the items in this book may not, at first, seem like art. Some may even have had a practical function. But decoration on everyday objects gives them additional value, which can signify a person's status, give a personal meaning to their owners, or display the skill of the maker. Around the world, many different things are considered art, and decoration can take many different forms.

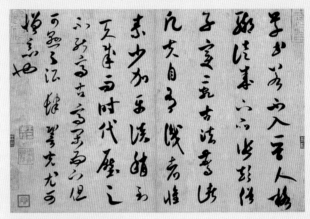

Chinese calligraphy

While countries in Europe and the US have traditionally valued paintings and sculpture, artists in China have long considered calligraphy a far more important art form. This manuscript, an essay on calligraphy styles, was written by Mi Fu, a painter, calligrapher, and poet of the Song Dynasty.

Arabic decoration

Much like China, the Islamic world has also prized calligraphy for centuries. In this 10th-century ceramic bowl from Iran, Kufic (early Arabic) lettering around the rim forms a beautiful, well-balanced pattern.

The inscription talks about the importance of planning before taking action.

Four-cornered hat

Hats like this finely woven and colorful example are usually associated with the ancient Wari and Tiwanaku cultures of South America. Those with intricate details such as animals and plants (as shown here) were reserved for men of high rank to show off their power.

A page from the Blue Quran

Rare Quran

Parchment dyed with indigo and decorated with gold lettering make the Blue Quran one of the most unusual Islamic manuscripts of the Medieval period. It was created in Tunisia, North Africa, and may have been inspired by the purple-dyed, gilded manuscripts of the Byzantine Empire.

c. 907–1125

Seated figure

This large Chinese sculpture is of Guanyin, a Buddhist *bodhisattva* (person on the path to enlightenment) who helps people in distress. At nearly 8 ft (2.5 m) high, it was carved from a single tree trunk, and then painted and gilded.

Guanyin of the Southern Sea

Beads made of rock crystal and glass catch the light.

The draped arm and relaxed pose convey the deity's regal calm.

900

c. 900

Painted pottery

The Indigenous Hohokam people, known today as the Tohono O'odham, Pima, and Pueblo Indians, flourished in what is now Arizona and in northern Mexico. Their pottery was usually made of buff or light brown clay. The objects were decorated with designs in red pigments, as seen in the repeating geometric pattern on this jar.

Hohokam jar

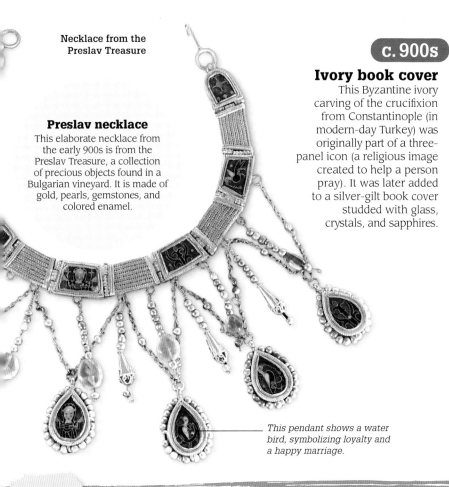

Necklace from the
Preslav Treasure

Preslav necklace
This elaborate necklace from the early 900s is from the Preslav Treasure, a collection of precious objects found in a Bulgarian vineyard. It is made of gold, pearls, gemstones, and colored enamel.

This pendant shows a water bird, symbolizing loyalty and a happy marriage.

c. 900s

Ivory book cover
This Byzantine ivory carving of the crucifixion from Constantinople (in modern-day Turkey) was originally part of a three-panel icon (a religious image created to help a person pray). It was later added to a silver-gilt book cover studded with glass, crystals, and sapphires.

Book cover with
ivory carving

950   **1000**

c. 950

Illuminated manuscript
The *Escorial Beatus* is an illustrated version of an earlier book, *Commentary on the Apocalypse*, written by the Spanish monk Beatus of Liébana. The unknown artist depicts scenes of the end of the world in the colorful Mozarabic style, which blends Christian and Islamic art.

Escorial Beatus

PARCHMENT

Invented in ancient Greece, parchment is a material used for writing. It is made from the skins of animals—primarily sheep, calves, and goats—that have been cleaned, stretched, and then dried to form a thin yet strong surface. Vellum is a finer quality parchment made using calfskin.

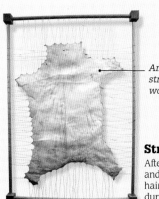

Animal skin stretched on a wooden frame

Manuscripts
Before the invention of machine printing, documents and books were made by hand. These are called manuscripts. Highly skilled scribes copied the text onto parchment, and sometimes added beautiful decorations called illuminations.

Stretching the parchment
After cleaning, the wet animal skins are stretched and scraped with a knife to remove any remaining hair or flesh. They are then dried to give a smooth, durable surface for writing.

Children in art

Children feature in art from all around the world, and although their clothes and hairstyles may differ, the things they are doing are much the same: playing, learning, and being at home. Some pictures feature children alone, while others show them with their family or friends. Whatever the time or place, the children are lively and having fun, or are absorbed in the moment, rarely caring about who is watching them.

Caring for pets, c. 450–440 BCE

Ancient Greek memorials often show children with their pet animals. This carved gravestone from Paros, an island famous for its marble sculptors, depicts the tender relationship between a girl and her doves. The carving is also known for the remarkable detail in the girl's hair and robes.

Family portrait, 1555

Italian artist Sofonisba Anguissola made many paintings of her family. In *The Chess Game*, three of her sisters are seen playing chess, watched over by their governess. It was unusual at this time for girls to play chess and shows that the sisters were educated. Each has a different expression and pose, revealing their individual characters.

The eldest sister looks at the viewer as she makes the winning move.

The artist skillfully captures the sheen on the textured fabric.

Friends at school, c. 1524–1525

This manuscript page, called *Laila and Majnun in School*, depicts a scene from a Persian poem. Made by the 16th-century Persian artist Shaikh Zada, it shows childhood sweethearts Laila and Majnun (center, holding hands) sharing a tender moment, among classmates who are reading, writing, and playing.

Dressing-up games, c. 1850–1889

In *Children at Play*, Japanese artist Kawanabe Kyosai illustrates a group of children playing a game of *kotori*, where one child puts on a mask and tries to catch the others. The expertly drawn faces of the children show both panic and excitement as they leap about, afraid of being caught.

Don't fall down! 1872

US artist Winslow Homer's *Snap the Whip* shows schoolboys using teamwork and strength to pull each other in opposite directions, while trying not to fall. The colorful and lively painting celebrates carefree country life, at a time when more and more people were moving to the cities.

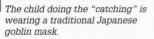

The child doing the "catching" is wearing a traditional Japanese goblin mask.

Loving family, 1973

Adults and children dance together in the bronze sculpture *Happy Children* by US artist Chaim Gross. Happy families were a favorite subject for this artist. Gross makes the adults much larger here, emphasizing their protective role, while a circle around the figures symbolizes the safety offered by a family.

Tired or bored? c. 1878

In *Little Girl in a Blue Armchair*, US Impressionist artist Mary Cassatt paints a girl on a comfortable armchair, perhaps bored or tired after playing. Her sprawling pose is unusual—children at this time were taught to sit up straight—and shows that she is either unaware or unconcerned that she is being watched.

The children are imitating the movements of the adults.

Temple portrait

Found inside the Brihadisvara Temple in Thanjavur, this mural is one of the earliest-known paintings of the Chola Dynasty of south India. It depicts the powerful King Rajaraja I (on the right) alongside his guru (spiritual teacher). They wear their hair piled on top of their heads, imitating the Hindu God Shiva.

Artists used natural pigments such as ocher, made from clay.

Portrait of King Rajaraja I and his guru

Sweet dreams
Chinese ceramic pillows were believed to bring good luck and ward off evil spirits. This one, dating from the Song Dynasty, takes the form of a happy, healthy boy, and may have belonged to a family wishing to produce a male heir.

1000

1050

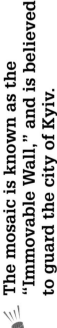

The mosaic is known as the "Immovable Wall," and is believed to guard the city of Kyiv.

c. 1000–1100

Cathedral mosaic

Dominating the interior of the Cathedral of St. Sophia in Kyiv, Ukraine, this dazzling 20-ft- (6-m-) high mosaic of the Virgin Mary at prayer is composed of around 2 million tiny mosaic tiles. It is regarded as one of the masterpieces of Byzantine art.

The scarlet slippers of the Virgin Mary stand out against her bright blue robe.

The Virgin Orans

1072

Mystical mountain

This dramatic scene of a mist-cloaked mountain by artist Guo Xi is a famous example of the *shan shui* style of Chinese painting, which depicted idealized landscapes using brush and ink. Scenes like this were intended to inspire calm contemplation.

Early Spring

Golden rhinoceros of Mapungubwe

c. 1075–1220

Golden hoard

This 6-in- (15-cm-) long figure of a rhinoceros was found in a burial site in what was once the Kingdom of Mapungubwe (in modern-day South Africa). It was one of a small number of animals found, although its purpose is unknown.

The gold foil once covered a wooden mold, now rotted away.

1100

1000–1150   ROMANESQUE ART

Taking inspiration from the Romans, whose ruined buildings were scattered all over the continent, a new style of art and architecture spread across medieval Europe, known as Romanesque. Massive stone churches were built, decorated with colorful murals and (later) stained-glass windows. These were designed to teach Bible stories to people who could not read.

Rounded arches echo the style of those used in ancient Roman buildings.

Impressive scale

With its massive, echoing spaces and solid stone construction, the 11th-century Maria Laach Abbey in Germany is considered a Romanesque masterpiece. The plain interior is broken up by brightly painted murals.

Miniature manuscript

This illustration is from the *Madrid Codex*, an 11th-century manuscript. It shows Rothari, king of the Lombards, sitting on his throne, in a typically Romanesque building with rounded arches.

45

UBI HAROLD·SACRAMENTVM·FE
VVILLELMO·DVCI·∶

The story
of a conquest

The Bayeux Tapestry, 11th century, Unknown artists

A 230-ft- (70-m-) long embroidery, skillfully stitched using dyed wools, the Bayeux Tapestry tells the epic story of the events leading up to the conquest of England by William, Duke of Normandy (a region of northern France) in 1066. Like a comic strip, it is a series of action-packed scenes shown in a continuous sequence. Full of fascinating details, this unique Romanesque artwork provides valuable insights into life in 11th-century Europe.

William of Normandy

The story is told from the point of view of William. He claimed to have been promised the English throne on the death of the king, Edward the Confessor.

Animal parade

The upper and lower sections of the tapestry are filled with images of animals. Some are drawn from real life, while others are imaginary beasts.

hIC HAROLD:DVX·:·

Harold swears an oath

The powerful noble Harold Godwinson promises to honor William's right to the English throne, but later returns home to claim it for himself. When the Normans invade, he is killed in an action-packed battle.

Holy bones

Harold swears his oath by touching caskets of holy relics. These relics were believed to be the remains of Christian saints, and by breaking his promise, Harold is shown to be going against God's wishes.

Sailing back to England

The ships in the tapestry are richly detailed and vividly colored. All are Viking-style "longships"— the Vikings were the foremost sea traders at this time, and both the Normans and the English copied their designs. In this scene, Harold returns to England after receiving William's blessing.

1100 ▶ 1200

Virgin of Vladimir

c. 1125

Miracle worker

This Byzantine icon of the Virgin and Child was made in Constantinople (present-day Istanbul, Turkey) and brought to the city of Vladimir in Russia. It was credited with protecting the country from a Mongol invasion, and became a famous national treasure.

1150–1175

Viking chess pieces

These chess pieces, carved from walrus ivory, were found on the Isle of Lewis in Scotland. The Vikings had settled in this area in the 9th century, and these characterful and intricately detailed objects reveal their skill in carving, as well as the games they enjoyed.

The Lewis chessmen

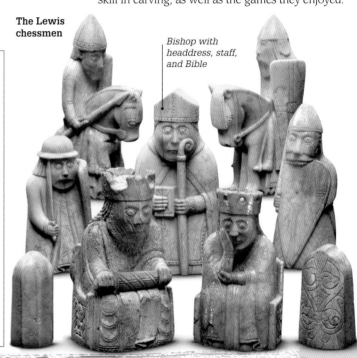

Bishop with headdress, staff, and Bible

1100　　　　　　　　　　　　　　　　　　　**1150**

THE ART OF STORYTELLING

Around the world, people have used pictures, sometimes combined with text, to tell religious stories and record important events in beautifully decorated manuscripts. Japan in particular had a rich tradition of *emaki*—handscrolls that could be unrolled one scene at a time. The illustrations in these manuscripts helped people understand the stories being told, just like comics and graphic novels today.

Recording Byzantine history

The *Madrid Skylitzes* is an illuminated manuscript (see p.41) from the 12th century that records the reigns of the Byzantine emperors. This scene shows a Byzantine ship attacking an enemy ship using Greek fire, a terrifying flame-throwing weapon.

Protecting Kyoto

The Tale of Great Minister Ban, a 66-ft- (20-m-) long handscroll (*emaki*) painted by Japanese artist Mitsunaga Kasuga in the late 12th century, tells the story of the destruction of Kyoto's imperial palace gate in 866. This scene shows people fighting the flames and eventually arresting the culprit.

The metal plaque has also been gilded.

Plaque with Censing Angels

1170–1180

Ornate plaque

The city of Limoges, France, was famous during the Medieval period for its elaborate enamels—metal objects decorated with colorful glass segments. This plaque was once situated at the top of an altar cross, and the serious expressions of the two angels with censers (incense burners) indicate that they are witnessing the Crucifixion of Christ.

1200

Chancay pottery

The pottery of the Chancay people of Peru had a distinctive black-on-white painting style, as in this 11th-century llama figurine. Llamas were important across South America, for transportation, clothing, and food.

The tilted head makes the llama appear as if it is watching something intently.

1150–1600   GOTHIC ART

The Gothic style started in northern France as a new way of designing churches, using slim pillars, rather than thick walls, to support the weight of the roof. Builders could now create taller buildings, which allowed space for larger windows and more decoration. The Gothic style came to be known for its elegance and elaborate design, and soon spread to arts such as painting and sculpture.

Religious art
Gothic art was strongly linked to Christianity. This ivory diptych (a two-paneled object that can be opened or closed during prayers) from France was made c. 1260–1270 and shows the Virgin Mary being crowned in heaven on the left, and the Last Judgment on the right.

The pointed shape is easier to make taller or wider.

Changing styles
The rounded arches and windows of the Romanesque style (see p.45) became pointed in the Gothic era, as seen in Barcelona Cathedral in Spain.

Grotesque sculptures
The exteriors of Gothic cathedrals and churches were often decorated with "grotesques"—carvings of monstrous creatures, such as this one from Lincoln Cathedral in England. These were thought to protect the building from evil spirits. Similar carvings called gargoyles functioned as waterspouts, draining rainwater away from the walls.

49

c. 1000–1300

Burning incense

In the medieval Islamic world, incense burners were used in royal courts or on special occasions to spread perfumed smoke. This bronze burner from Iran has been skillfully shaped like a bird. Its belly contains a small bowl to hold the incense. When lit, the smoke would seep through the decorative holes in its body.

Rooster-shaped incense burner from Iran

c. 1240

Illuminated Bible

The Crusader Bible is one of the most famous illuminated manuscripts in the world. Its miniatures depict people and events from the Old Testament but set in 13th-century France. The illustrations contain bold colors, and show intricate details of the clothing and armor of the period.

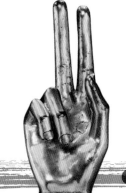

A page from the Crusader Bible

1200

c. 1200s

Medieval beast

The ferocious lion's face looks almost human in this fresco from a Romanesque monastery in northern Spain. The artist may never have seen a real lion, but has nevertheless managed to capture its nature, with a raised tail and back leg muscles tensed as if it is ready to pounce.

Interlocking fish make a decorative border motif.

Lion fresco from Spain

c. 1230

Holy bones

This unusual object is a reliquary, something to hold religious relics (usually bones or bone fragments of saints). It is not certain that these relics were genuine, but people often traveled great distances to see them. Reliquaries were often shaped like the body part they contained—this one from the Netherlands, made from precious metals and jewels, probably held arm bones. These could be viewed through the holes in the side.

Arm reliquary

c. 1250–1299

Storming a city

The Tale of Heiji is a 23-ft- (7-m-) long illustrated manuscript (*emaki*—see p.48) that depicts events from a short civil war in Japan during the 12th century. It features detailed depictions of buildings and clothing styles of the period. This section shows flames engulfing the emperor's palace during an attack, brilliantly capturing the chaos of battle.

Events unfold from right to left.

Night Attack on the Sanjo Palace, from *The Tale of Heiji*

Seated terra-cotta figurine

1200s

West African sculpture

This terra-cotta figure is from Djenné-Djenno, which was an important craft and trade center of the ancient Mali Empire of West Africa. The sculpture shows an anxious figure, who sits hugging their leg. The significance of the bumps along the back is unknown, but they may be symptoms of a disease.

1250 ———————————•———————————•——————————— 1300 ▶▶

ART FOR WORSHIP

Icons are religious artwork for people to think about while praying. Most Christian icons from the Middle Ages show elongated figures on flat, gold backgrounds. Islamic artists used patterns and verses from the Quran for the viewer to contemplate, because the use of human forms for worship is forbidden in Islam.

The first saints

Christian icons depict Jesus, Mary, or saints, usually against a gilded background that symbolizes heaven. This icon from Kievan Rus (in present-day Eastern Europe) shows the brothers Boris and Gleb, the region's first Christian saints.

Mixtec vessel

This clay vessel is from the Mixtec people, and was found in Zaachila, Mexico. It was made sometime between 1000–1400, and its skeletal handle probably represents Mictlantecuhtli—the god of death.

Tomb tile

This intricately decorated tile from 1334 comes from a tomb complex in Qom, Iran. Islamic religious sites are often decorated with glazed tiles. They feature elaborate designs of natural shapes, such as flowers or stars, or calligraphy of words from the Quran.

A section of the *Tonindeye Codex*

History in pictures

A codex is a type of ancient manuscript that was used to record history or important events. This busy and colorful scene is part of a codex called *Tonindeye*, which means "story of the people." Using pictures rather than words, it shows us the family relationships and battle victories of Eight Deer Jaguar-Claw, the 11th-century ruler of the Mixtec people of Mexico. Depicted at the very center of the scene is a temple. The leader himself is shown top right, gambling for the town of Tutupec. The section on the left shows the birth of Lady 1 Death, who will begin a new dynasty.

Mixtec means
**"inhabitants of
the Place of the
Clouds"** in Nahuatl,
a language of
the region.

1300 ▸ 1400

The decorative crown features a rosette.

Head of an Oni

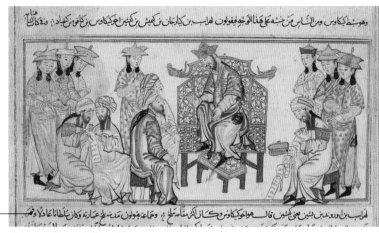

This calligraphy is Arabic, but there was also a version in Persian.

Compendium of Chronicles

Early 1300s

Sculptures from Ife

The Kingdom of Ife flourished between the 12th and 15th centuries in what is now Nigeria. Artists from Ife created remarkably lifelike brass and bronze busts, such as this one of an *oni* (ruler). To date, 19 of these have been found. This sculpture probably shows a female *oni*.

1314

Mongol history

By the 1300s, the Mongols were beginning to tell their own stories as conquerors of Asia. The *Compendium of Chronicles* (*Jami al-tawarikh*), by Persian historian Rashid al-Din, is a world history, but is filled with accounts of Mongol military victories. It contains intricate calligraphy and illustrations made by hundreds of artists.

c. 1267–1337   GIOTTO DI BONDONE

The Italian artist known as Giotto sparked an enormous change in Western art. The Byzantine style of the time was flat and stylized, but Giotto began painting people and places more as they appeared in real life, using accurate proportions, facial expressions, light and shadow, and details such as folds in fabric to make them seem three-dimensional.

1300

1320

Jewish prayer book

The Haggadah, which is a Jewish book read during the Passover meal, describes how the Israelites escaped slavery in Egypt. The Golden Haggadah from Spain is one of the most luxurious versions, featuring detailed miniature illustrations from the story set on a gold leaf background.

The gilded background would have shimmered in the candlelight.

Majestic representation

In the early 1300s, Giotto made the *Ognissanti Madonna* for the Ognissanti (All Saints) church in Florence, Italy. It is an example of *maestà* (meaning "majesty"), a representation of an enthroned Mary and a young Jesus with angels and saints. Giotto's figures all have varying proportions, expressions, and gestures, which make them look unusually real.

Golden Haggadah

This figure is 4⅓ in (11 cm) tall.

Aztec warrior ornament

c. 1325

Celebrating warriors

Warfare was important to the Aztecs, who lived in what is modern-day Mexico. The elaborate jewelery and weapons on this Aztec figure suggest that he is an elite Aztec warrior. The ornament is made from gold and silver, and may have been worn as a pendant or attached to clothes.

The figure holds a shield, darts, and a dart thrower.

Painting nature

This early 14th-century handscroll painting from China's Yuan Dynasty was created by the artist Xie Chufang. It is an example of *caochong* art, which depicts plants and insects, and shows how skilled he was in capturing the natural world.

Fascination of Nature

1400

Spanish colonists looted many Aztec gold artifacts and melted them down to use the valuable metal for other purposes.

Each figure holds a book, which is a symbol of their individual Gospel.

c. 1330

Gospel book

In c. 300 CE, Armenia became the first country to adopt Christianity as an official religion. This page from a rare Gospel book made in Armenia shows the four Gospel authors—Matthew, Mark, Luke, and John—in colorful clothing that may be similar to that worn by Armenian clergymen of the time.

Leaf from a Gospel book with the four authors

1400–1600

This period saw the Renaissance—a "rebirth" of culture—in Europe. Artists found groundbreaking ways to make their paintings and sculptures more realistic, reviving forgotten ideas from ancient Greece and Rome. The development of printing meant that art and illustrated books could now be seen and owned by more people. In Asia, art continued to be influenced by religious philosophies such as Sufism and Buddhism. Increase in trade from the East inspired the creation of beautiful objects, such as the Chinese silk paintings and porcelain vessels sold in markets around the world.

The Great East Window, York Minster, England

This embroidery was made using silk and metallic threads.

The lion is shown with its mouth open to appear more ferocious.

Embroidered lion badge from Ming China

c. 1400s

Status symbols

Embroidery was an important art form in Ming Dynasty China. The silk robes of government officials were embroidered with animals, both real and mythical, to represent the wearer's rank. The lion symbolized the second-highest status in the military.

1400

1405–1408

Medieval stained glass

This magnificent window is the largest piece of medieval stained glass in England. It was made for York Minster (a Gothic cathedral) by John Thornton, and is 78 ft (24 m) tall—about the size of a tennis court. The window consists of 311 panels showing scenes from the Bible, from creation to the end of times.

Feathered headdress

Featherwork was central to the art of the Aztecs of Mexico. Feathers were used to decorate shields, headdresses, and cloaks. Only the emperor and important warriors wore these status symbols.

Early 1400s

Chinese porcelain

Blue-and-white Chinese porcelain from the Ming Dynasty period was highly sought after, particularly in Europe. This jar was made in Jingdezhen, the "porcelain capital" of northern China. It is decorated with a cobalt blue dragon, a common motif in Chinese art. Dragons represent power and luck in Chinese belief.

The claws on dragon motifs stood for the owner's social rank, and high ranks were shown with a larger number of claws.

Porcelain jar from Ming Dynasty China

> **"He alone ... brought sculpture back to marvelous perfection in our age."**
>
> Giorgio Vasari on Donatello, *Lives of the Artists*, 1568

c. 1415–1417

Bold protector

Donatello was one of the greatest sculptors of the early Italian Renaissance, a period of discoveries and new artistic styles. His sculpture of St. George was commissioned by a church in Florence, Italy. St. George was a hero and protector figure of the city, and so Donatello portrays him as a strong, youthful man wearing armor, with a determined expression and posture.

St. George

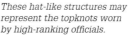

1420

These hat-like structures may represent the topknots worn by high-ranking officials.

c. 1100–1650

Colossal statues

On Easter Island (Rapa Nui), off the South American mainland, nearly 1,000 colossal stone figures known as Moai stand along the coast. They were made by the Indigenous Rapa Nui people. The statues were probably tied with ropes and "walked" across the island to their positions by pulling from side to side. The largest one is 72 ft (22 m) tall and weighs more than 176 tons (160 metric tons).

The statues stand with their backs to the sea, keeping watch over the islanders.

Moai of Easter Island

Myths and sacred stories

Every culture has stories that are passed from generation to generation, some of which are central to their religion. Many of these stories are about the triumph of good over evil, and often feature fantastical creatures, acts of heroism, and examples of bravery, loyalty, and determination. Other tales explain the world through the actions of gods and goddesses. Artists return to these myths and sacred stories over and over, retelling them in new ways.

The sculpture is 16ft (5m) high.

A dangerous trap, 480 BCE
This red-and-black vase from ancient Greece illustrates a scene from *The Odyssey*, an epic poem by the Greek poet Homer. It shows sirens—mythical creatures that are half-bird, half-woman—who sing in an effort to lure the ship of the hero Odysseus toward dangerous rocks in order to wreck it. Odysseus is tied to the ship's mast to resist the song of the sirens.

Lucky charm, c. 907–1125 CE
In Chinese mythology, a creature called a phoenix is connected with good fortune and immortality. People believed that wearing phoenix symbols would bring them good luck. This pendant from the Liao Dynasty is carved from white jade—also considered lucky!

Lion-tamer king, 721–705 BCE
Gilgamesh was a legendary king of Mesopotamia (modern-day Iraq) and the hero of one of the world's oldest written stories, *The Epic of Gilgamesh*. This imposing relief, found at the ruins of King Sargon II's palace, may represent Gilgamesh, towering over a lion he has overpowered.

The knight and the dragon, c. 1470
George of Lydda, a Christian saint, was a popular subject among medieval European artists. In his dreamlike painting *St. George and the Dragon*, Italian artist Paolo Uccello shows the saint dressed as a brave knight, killing a snarling dragon to save a princess.

Fighting demons, 1649–1653

This lively painting is from an illustrated version of the *Ramayana*, an ancient Hindu epic poem about the struggle between good and evil. It shows a battle between the monkey army of Prince Rama and the demon forces of the many-headed Ravana, who has captured Rama's wife, Sita. The battle is brought to life in rich detail by Sahībdīn, a renowned painter of the Mewar school of painting from Rajasthan, India.

God of thunder, 1872

In *Thor's Fight with the Giants*, Swedish painter Mårten Winge presents Thor, the Norse god of thunder, as a force for good. A radiant Thor descends from the sky on his chariot, toppling evil giants with thunderbolts from his mighty hammer.

River goddess, c. 1960

Nigerian artist Twins Seven-Seven uses colors and patterns inspired by traditional textiles to paint the stories and practices of the Yoruba culture. In *The Fisherman and the River Goddess with His Captured Multi-Colored Fishes and the River Night Guard*, the Yoruba goddess Oshun is shown on a boat with a fisherman and some fish.

In the third panel, Noah and his family emerge from the Ark after the Flood.

Baptistery doors

The eyes are made from mother of pearl.

Mask of Xiuhtecuhtli

1425–1452

Gilded masterpiece

Italian sculptor Lorenzo Ghiberti took 27 years to make these doors for the Baptistery of San Giovanni, a religious building in Florence. Each of the 10 gilded bronze panels shows a story from the Old Testament of the Bible. Fellow artist Michelangelo was so impressed that he called the doors the "Gates of Paradise."

1420

c. 1400–1521

Turquoise mask

In the Aztec culture of central Mexico, Xiuhtecuhtli was the god of fire, who was linked to creation. This mask, made of tiny fragments of the mineral turquoise, is a representation of him. It may have been used in religious ceremonies or royal burials.

1400s–1500s   CHANGING STYLES

While the Medieval era had been a time of hardship, a new period known as the Renaissance brought hope, beauty, and new knowledge, in part by studying ancient Greece and Rome. This new culture was reflected in the change in artistic styles— as shown in these two contrasting paintings of the same subject, but from the two different periods.

Medieval art
The subject matter in Medieval art was more important than technique or style. Works of art often focused on religion. The paintings of the time were typically dark and serious, with flat, unrealistic proportions, and used a limited range of colors. This can be seen in Italian artist Berlinghiero's *Madonna and Child*, with its unrealistic hands and long fingers.

Renaissance art
Renaissance art brought a sense of three dimensions to a flat surface with the use of perspective (see p.79). In *Madonna of the Meadow* (1506) by Raphael, the Madonna is much more realistic and painted in bright colors.

1433

A self-portrait?

Flemish artist Jan van Eyck was one of the first in northwestern Europe to produce realistic paintings during the Renaissance, skillfully capturing minute details in his works. The man in this picture is believed to be van Eyck himself. He has tied up his chaperon (a type of hood) to stop it from getting dirty while he is painting.

Portrait of a Man

OIL PAINTING

Although oil paints had been used for hundreds of years, it was Jan van Eyck who came up with a recipe that helped his brilliant colors shine. Oils can be built up in layers, called glazes, to give the painting a feeling of depth.

Blending colors
Oil paints are bright and transparent. Artists use a flat board called a palette to blend different colors together before painting.

Brush strokes
Oil paints can be used in thick daubs using a large brush, or in delicate strokes using a smaller one.

1430

1440

1430–1440

Raising a storm

Some of the most beautiful examples of Persian art of this period are found in this illustrated copy of the 10th-century epic poem *The Book of Kings* (*Shahnameh*) by the poet Firdausi. It features myths and historical stories from Persia (modern-day Iran). In this scene, a sorcerer conjures up a storm to confuse Persian soldiers.

 This painting was probably made in a workshop in northern India that had artists from various parts of India and Persia.

Bazur, the Magician, Raises up Darkness and a Storm

The Adoration of the Shepherds

Andrea Mantegna was a carpenter's son, and became an apprentice to a painter at the age of about 11.

c. 1450

Homage to Jesus

Shepherds visiting the baby Jesus to pay their respects is a popular theme in Christian art. Italian artist Andrea Mantegna has depicted Joseph, baby Jesus, and the shepherds here as dark skinned, a more realistic representation of their Middle Eastern origin than was usual at the time.

1440 — 1445 — 1450

Calligraphic jade cup

1442–1445

Clay with a glaze

Italian sculptor Luca della Robbia invented a technique using tin glaze that gave terra-cotta a polished look, as seen here on the figures of Robbia's sculpture from Florence Cathedral, Italy. The white against the cobalt blue of the sky suggests purity and spirituality.

Inca textile

In the Inca Empire of Peru, textiles were highly valued possessions, symbolizing wealth and status. Finely woven by hand, the best were more prized than gold and silver. This *uncu* (tunic) from c. 1450–1550, was made to adorn a figurine.

1447–1449

Precious cup

This rare white jade cup from Asia's Timurid Empire is just 1 in (2.5 cm) tall and 2 in (5 cm) wide. Expertly carved calligraphy decorates its body. The Arabic inscription around the center says the cup was commissioned by Timurid ruler Ala ud-Daulah, while the Persian writing on the rim indicates it later belonged to India's Mughal emperor Jahangir.

The Resurrection

Tunic made of animal hair

1454
Daoist art
This ink painting on a silk scroll was commissioned from an unknown artist by a Ming Dynasty emperor in China. It depicts two groups of star deities (gods) of the Daoist religion. Each group represents a constellation or "dipper." They are saving all beings from going to hell. The names of the deities are written in gold on the right-hand side.

This group is wearing royal robes, while the other is dressed more plainly.

Star deities of the northern and central dippers

c. 1400–1599
Ivory carving
Ivory carvers in West Africa made artifacts for Benin's *oba* (king) and other royal courts. When the Portuguese arrived in the region, they were so impressed by the carvers' skill that they commissioned items to take back to European royal households. These artifacts are known as "West African Luso ivories," and they often incorporate both European and West African motifs, as seen in this elaborate salt cellar.

A stylized rose topped with an acorn lid is a European motif.

Ivory salt cellar

1455

1460 ▶▶

c. 1430s   PRINTING AND ART

The use of the printing press in Europe in the 15th century not only revolutionized the spread of knowledge but also helped art reach a wider audience. Pictures could now be printed at a lower cost, and in larger numbers, making it possible for the poor to buy items such as devotional images.

Early printing processes
Early printers used two methods. Woodcuts used a raised surface (relief) that was covered in ink. Intaglio was where lines were carved into a metal plate that held the ink.

Many images were colored by hand with watercolors after they had been printed.

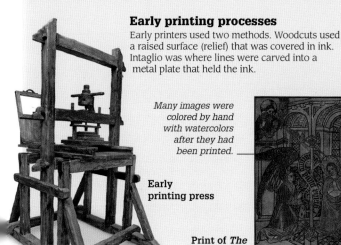

Early printing press

Print of *The Annunciation*

The dogs snarl at the snakes.

Snakes hang down menacingly

A woman in an African dress stands close to a warrior with a shield and a sword.

Ray of light

God and His angels watch from above. A ray of light, representing God's power and an act of creation, reaches down to Mary. She now bears a child who will become the baby Jesus.

Dove

The dove is a symbol of the Holy Spirit in Christian art. It is often seen in paintings of the Annunciation. Here we see the dove flying down from Heaven on a ray of light directly to Mary.

Lily

The white lily represents purity and is used almost exclusively in paintings of the Annunciation to represent Mary. The lily also blooms in spring—the season associated with new life.

Peacock feathers

In Christian art, peacock feathers are a sign of immortality and are often used for the wings of angels, the heavenly messengers of God. The "eyes" in the peacock feathers represent God's ability to see everything.

A divine message

Annunciation, 1443–1450, Filippo Lippi

Italian artist Filippo Lippi was known for the intricate details of his paintings, such as carefully drawn folds in clothing and expressive faces. He also used perspective to create the look of a real, three-dimensional world on a flat surface. Lippi's great skill is seen in this painting of the Annunciation, a popular subject in Christian art, in which the angel Gabriel tells the Virgin Mary that she will be the mother of a child—the Son of God.

Halo

A halo, depicted here by a radiant disk around the head, is a symbol of holiness in Christian art. It tells the viewer that they are looking at a person of great virtue and importance. The Virgin Mary has a halo as she is believed to be holy.

Blue robes

Blue paint was very expensive, as its ingredients included crushed lapis lazuli, a valuable gemstone. Lippi has used it for the robes on Mary and God, indicating that they are the most important figures in the painting.

Prayer book

Paintings of the Annunciation usually depict Mary reading a prayer book when she is interrupted by the angel Gabriel. This is meant to show her devotion to God, and relates to a Medieval belief that she was educated as a scholar in ancient Jerusalem.

1400–1500   POWERFUL WOMEN

Since the 14th century, it had been popular for European artists to depict female characters as strong and dominant, in order to challenge accepted views of the role of women in a male-dominated society. In Germany, this style of art was called *Weibermacht*, which means "power of women." In the 15th century, artists particularly focused on Biblical figures, such as Judith and Delilah, who defied expectations with their brave and violent deeds.

Warrior woman
Judith was a Jewish heroine of the Old Testament. Sandro Botticelli's *The Return of Judith to Bethulia* (1472) shows Judith carrying the sword she used to kill the enemy general Holofernes, as well as an olive branch symbolizing peace. Her maid, Abra, follows with Holofernes's head.

Tricking a hero
In *Samson and Delilah* (1495–1500), Italian painter Andrea Mantegna shows Delilah cutting the hair of the hero Samson as he lies asleep. Delilah had tricked Samson into revealing that his hair gave him superhuman strength. The grapevine around the tree symbolizes Samson's drunken slumber, which leaves him powerless against Delilah. This style of painting, which uses mostly shades of gray, is called "grisaille."

Korean portrait
Portrait artists in Korea traditionally painted their subjects in a full-length seated position. Artists took particular care with the details of the subject's face because they revealed important information. This portrait by an unknown artist shows Sin Suk-ju, a highly respected scholar and politician during the Joseon Dynasty.

The bright, clear eyes show wisdom and nobility.

Portrait of Sin Suk-ju

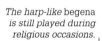

1460

Combining cultures
The Bible tells how King David would play his harp to ward off evil. This depiction, made in the mid-1400s by an Italian monk in Ethiopia, gives the story a local feel by showing David playing an Ethiopian instrument called a *begena*.

The harp-like begena is still played during religious occasions.

This figure is shown at a smaller scale because he is less important.

Poet on a Mountain Top

c. 1480
Sufi art
Islamic mystics, called Sufis or Dervishes, perform the *sama* (a spiritual dance) in this colorful miniature painting by the Persian artist Bihzad. Sufis believed that by playing music, dancing, and reciting a prayer, they could enter a trance, allowing them to clear their minds and get closer to Allah (God).

Dancing Dervishes

The poem recreates the artist's feelings when read aloud.

c. 1471
Expressing emotions
Poet on a Mountain Top by Shen Zhou is an example of Chinese literati painting. This art style focuses on the artist's emotional state or feelings instead of realistic scenes. In this painting, the small human figure on top of the mountain symbolizes how insignificant a person feels compared to the forces of nature.

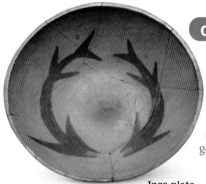

c. 1450–1532
Inca artifact
This simple but elegant plate, decorated with a drawing of two fish, was made by an unknown Inca artist from what is now Peru. Most Inca pottery was made for domestic use, but vessels meant for ceremonies and rituals contained geometric or animal themes.

Inca plate

1470

1480 ▶▶

1477–1482
Welcoming spring
In *Primavera*, one of several large Renaissance works inspired by Classical mythology, Italian painter Sandro Botticelli represents the onset of spring. The Roman goddess of love, Venus, stands in the center. The Three Graces, who represent happiness, elegance, and beauty, dance in a circle, while the messenger god Mercury chases away winter clouds with a wand. On the right, the nymph (nature deity) Chloris transforms into Flora, the goddess of spring.

Primavera

Man in the mirror, 1434

Belgian artist Jan van Eyck was famous for his attention to detail. Look closely at the circular mirror behind the wealthy couple in *The Arnolfini Portrait*: it reflects two men, one of whom is thought to be the artist himself.

Among the best, 1509–1511

In his fresco *The School of Athens*, Italian Renaissance artist Raphael depicts the most brilliant minds of ancient Greece and Rome, as well as some great artists of his time. Raphael appears at the far right, looking straight at the viewer. By including himself among famous figures such as Greek philosophers Aristotle and Plato, and fellow Renaissance artists Leonardo da Vinci and Michelangelo, Raphael shows the utmost confidence in his talents.

The artist at work, 1656

In *The Ladies-in-Waiting*, Spanish court painter Diego Velázquez presents a realistic portrait of himself at work in the Royal Palace in Madrid. He may be painting the king and queen, who are visible in the mirror in the background.

Spot the artist!

There is a longstanding tradition of artists including themselves in their own works. In the earliest examples, they often did this so they could become better known. More recently, artists have disguised themselves in order to explore ideas about identity and self-expression. Whatever the reason, it can sometimes be a challenge to spot these masters of disguise.

Part of the nightlife, 1892–1895

French artist Henri de Toulouse-Lautrec is renowned for his lively paintings of Parisian nightlife. *At the Moulin Rouge* features guests enjoying an evening at the famous nightclub Moulin Rouge. The artist was very short due to a medical condition, and he draws attention to this by placing himself next to his tall cousin.

A ghost among the flowers, 2009

Peruvian artist Cecilia Paredes is known for using body paint in order to blend into patterned backgrounds, as in the photograph *Nocturne*. It is her way of exploring people's desire to fit in.

The artist as president, 2010

Artist Roger Shimomura likes to explore his Japanese-American identity. *Shimomura Crossing the Delaware* imitates the famous 19th-century painting *Washington Crossing the Delaware* (see p.132), but in the style of Japanese woodblock prints. By putting himself in the place of the first US president, George Washington, Shimomura asks what it means to be American.

1480 ▶ 1500

Painting showing the transportation of Chinese porcelain

c. 1480

Cultural exchange

The Silk Road allowed the exchange of goods between East and West. This Persian miniature painting celebrates the West Asian fascination with Chinese Ming porcelain. It shows the wedding procession of a Chinese princess. Large blue-and-white Ming vessels are among the bride's valued possessions.

1452–1519   LEONARDO DA VINCI

Born in Florence, Italy, Leonardo da Vinci was one of the most successful and respected artists of the Renaissance era (see p.62). He was not only a painter, but also a sculptor, architect, engineer, musician, and inventor. Da Vinci was centuries ahead of his time with his many groundbreaking ideas and skills.

Design for the Aerial Screw, a helicopter-like machine

The artist's notebooks
Da Vinci recorded his ideas, inventions, and experiments in several notebooks. He wrote his notes backward, from right to left, so that they could only be read when held up to a mirror, perhaps for secrecy.

1480

1490

Meleager is poised with a spear, ready to kill a monstrous boar.

Gilded bronzes
Italian sculptor Pier Bonacolsi was known for his small, detailed bronzes inspired by Classical sculptures. Bonacolsi often gilded his bronzes, as seen in this sculpture of the Greek mythical hero Meleager from the late 15th century.

Even the intricate sandals have been gilded, showing the artist's great skill.

Meleager

c. 1485

Botticelli's goddess

The Birth of Venus, by Italian painter Sandro Botticelli, shows the Roman goddess of love, Venus, emerging fully-grown from the sea. Minor gods blow her sea shell to shore and cover her with a cloak. The painting was admired for the floating, wind-blown effect of the figures.

The Birth of Venus

The Last Supper

c. 1495–1498

Announcing a betrayal

Italian painter Leonardo da Vinci's *The Last Supper*, a large wall painting 29 ft (9 m) wide, captures the moment when Jesus tells his Apostles (followers) that one of them will betray him. Da Vinci skillfully depicts a range of reactions to this news through the expressions and poses of the figures.

The faces of the Apostles show shock and disbelief as Jesus announces that one of them will betray him.

1500

1496

Showing devotion

This work by Japanese artist Sesshū Tōyō is quite different from earlier Japanese ink painting (see p.51) due to its thicker, heavier lines and detailed background. It shows a Buddhist monk, Huike, cutting off an arm as a sign of loyalty to Bodhidharma, the founder of Zen Buddhism.

Huike appeals to Bodhidharma, who faces the wall in zazen (sitting meditation), to accept him as a disciple.

Huike Offering His Arm to Bodhidharma

Female head

1400s

Yoruba art

Art by the Yoruba people of Nigeria is influenced by their religious beliefs, and many works are made to honor *orishas* (deities), who often help humans. This elegant head from the 1400s is thought to represent the *orisha* Queen Oronsen, who was also the wife of the Yoruba king, Rerengejen. Terra-cotta sculptures like these were usually made by women.

1500 ▶ 1520

c. 1500
Nature up close
Chinese artist Yin Hong is known for his skill in depicting fur and feathers. He was commissioned to make this silk scroll painting as a decoration for a Ming palace. Depictions of birds and flowers reflected the qualities of the emperor and his followers. Here, the pheasants symbolize the bravery of the emperor, while the partridges represent the faithfulness of his subjects.

Birds and Flowers of Early Spring

c. 1503–1519
An enigmatic smile
The *Mona Lisa*, a painting by the Italian artist Leonardo da Vinci (see p.72), has attracted discussion about the woman's identity and her mysterious smile. She is now thought to be Lisa Gherardini, a Florentine silk merchant's wife. Da Vinci captured her expression using a technique called *sfumato* (see p.79), where colors are blended into each other to create a lifelike image with a smokey, hazy effect. And the secret of her smile? The artist probably paid people to entertain her while he painted.

Mona Lisa

▶▶ 1500

1471–1528   ALBRECHT DÜRER

Albrecht Dürer was born in Nuremberg, now part of Germany. He is known for his extraordinarily detailed and realistic artwork. Dürer traveled widely, learning many skills, but his trips to Italy had the greatest influence on his work. He made more than 70 paintings, 100 engravings, and 200 woodcuts before he died.

Skillful detail
In *Young Hare* (1502), Dürer sketched an outline of the animal before applying a thin wash of watercolor. He then filled in the details of the hare's fur and whiskers using individual strokes of brown, black, white, and yellow paint.

"Simplicity is the ultimate sophistication."
Leonardo da Vinci, 1452–1519

Aztec mosaic

The serpent was a powerful symbol in Aztec culture, and this double-headed icon was worn during ceremonial rituals. Made sometime in the 1400s or 1500s, the wooden carving is covered in a mosaic of turquoise and red thorny oyster shell.

The sharp teeth are made from conch shell.

The Worship of Venus

For the Aztecs, serpents symbolized fertility and rebirth because they could shed their skin.

1518–1519

Paintings of a goddess

Italian artist Titian was known for his landscapes, portraits, and mythological scenes. In *The Worship of Venus*, he paints a ceremony to honor the Roman goddess Venus. As cupids gather apples, a symbol of the goddess, women make offerings to a statue of Venus. Set against a beautiful landscape, this celebration represents the fertility of women and nature.

1510

1520

c. 1500s

Intricate carving

This ivory carving from Ming China shows a female version of Guanyin, the *bodhisattva* of compassion (see p.40). Here, she is holding a child. This form of Guanyin was believed to have the power to bless people with children. The artist has expertly carved the statue out of a single piece of ivory, using the natural curve to show Guanyin balancing the child on her hip.

Cherubs look up at the serious scene.

The Sistine Madonna

1512–1513

Famous Madonna

The Sistine Madonna was one of the final paintings of Mary made by Italian artist Raphael. It shows Mary and the infant Jesus emerging from behind painted curtains, almost as if she is presenting the child to the viewer.

Bodhisattva Guanyin

An uncontrollable blaze

The Forest Fire, 1505, Piero di Cosimo

In one of the earliest Renaissance landscape paintings, Italian artist Piero di Cosimo depicts the two sides of nature—its beauty and its power to destroy. As a fire spreads rapidly through the lush forest, Piero captures the fear and confusion of the many different creatures. Even some of the people are in a panic as the terrible blaze reaches their homes. The painting is believed to have been inspired by a poem by the ancient philosopher and poet Lucretius, which describes how civilization began when people overcame their fear of fire and began to put it to good use.

Fleeing to safety

There is a sense of urgency among the birds as they fly away, some making their way to the tree in the foreground. Piero has painted many different species, including a peregrine falcon, a woodcock, a pigeon, an osprey, a rook, and a common crane.

Mythical animals

Just as he was finishing his painting, Piero added the faces of mythological creatures called satyrs onto the heads of a pig and a deer. This last-minute addition might have been a joke at the request of the person who commissioned this painting.

Approaching danger

In the distance, some people, presumably the cowherd's family, have rushed out of their home and are pointing at the burning forest in alarm, while others can be seen drawing water from a well to try to put out the fire.

Herdsman

Despite the advancing blaze, the cowherd calmly drives his cows to safety. Piero has used him to illustrate how people conquered fire and used it to work metals, shown here by the metal edge of the yoke on his shoulder.

Individual expressions

Piero was a very imaginative painter and gave the individual animals different expressions, showing his attention to detail. With her tongue lolling out, this cow bellows in alarm.

Fiery inferno

The way Piero has painted the forest fire is very dramatic. The white-hot sparks and orangey-red embers ripping through the trees show how hot the wildfire must be, turning the trees into exploding fireworks.

1520 ▶ 1540

Krishna and the Cowherds,
from the *Bhagavata Purana*

Frog necklace
These gold frog-shaped beads from c. 1500 were typically made into necklaces for Aztec and Mixtec nobles of modern-day Mexico. Frogs and turtles, which lay large numbers of eggs, were symbols of fertility.

1520–1530

Indian manuscript paintings
Krishna (the blue figure), the human form of Hindu God Vishnu, tends to his cattle in this scene from an illustrated version of the *Bhagavata Purana*, one of the earliest-known manuscripts from India. The work was created by a group of painters, and features flat backgrounds and figures in profile—styles that were popular at the time in Indian painting.

1520 **1530**

1520–1524

Meeting of saints
One of German artist Matthias Grünewald's finest works, this painting shows the meeting of two saints, one a religious leader from Europe (left) and the other a military leader from Africa (right). The lavish clothes and objects in the scene display the power and wealth of the Catholic Church.

*The Meeting of Saints
Erasmus and Maurice*

1440–1897   THE ART OF BENIN

The Kingdom of Benin was a city-state in what is now Nigeria. By the 15th century, Benin had become a wealthy nation that was known for its superbly crafted bronze statues and ivory carvings. Benin was invaded and colonized by the British in the 18th century, and its art was plundered for display in Europe and the US. Many of these priceless artifacts are now being returned.

Ivory mask
This 16th-century mask was made to honor the mother of an *oba* (king) of Benin. Artists of Benin worked only for the *oba*, and created elaborate objects for use in important ceremonies.

*Queen Mother
Pendant Mask*

Classical sculpture

Italian artist Michelangelo's bust of Brutus, one of Julius Caesar's assassins, was one of the first sculptures to revive the Classical style of ancient Rome. By sculpting Brutus, the enemy of a famous leader, Michelangelo was showing his anger toward the Medici family, the violent leaders of Florence at the time.

1540

Bust of Brutus

"Every block of stone has a statue inside it and it is the task of the sculptor to discover it."

Michelangelo, 1475–1564

RENAISSANCE PAINTING TECHNIQUES

Renaissance artists used several techniques to make their paintings more realistic. The most important were perspective, foreshortening, and proportion—all of which use mathematical principles—and *chiaroscuro* and *sfumato*, which play with color and shading. These techniques allowed the artists to create a sense of depth, giving their work a three-dimensional feel.

Sfumato and *chiaroscuro*

Italian artist Leonardo da Vinci's *Madonna of the Rocks* (1491–1508) shows two different techniques. *Sfumato*, which means "soft, natural shading," was created by da Vinci. He used it to blend the colors of the dark natural setting and the bright figures, creating a unique smoky effect. The artist has also used *chiaroscuro*, where highly contrasting light and shade create depth and atmosphere.

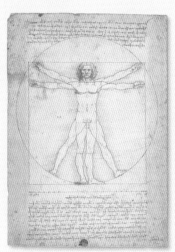

Proportion

Leonardo came up with a way to create realistic body proportions based on ideas from the ancient Greeks and Romans. In *Vitruvian Man* (c. 1490), he shows how a person's height should be equal to the length of their outstretched arms.

Foreshortening

In *Lamentation of Christ* (c. 1480), Italian artist Andrea Mantegna uses foreshortening to dramatic effect. The technique shows how a figure or object appears distorted when viewed from an unusual angle.

Perspective

In *The Tribute Money* (c. 1427), Italian painter Masaccio has used perspective to create the illusion of distance by placing the figures and buildings in lines that meet at a single spot, called the "vanishing point." Here, green lines have been marked to show how this spot is located on the central figure of Jesus Christ.

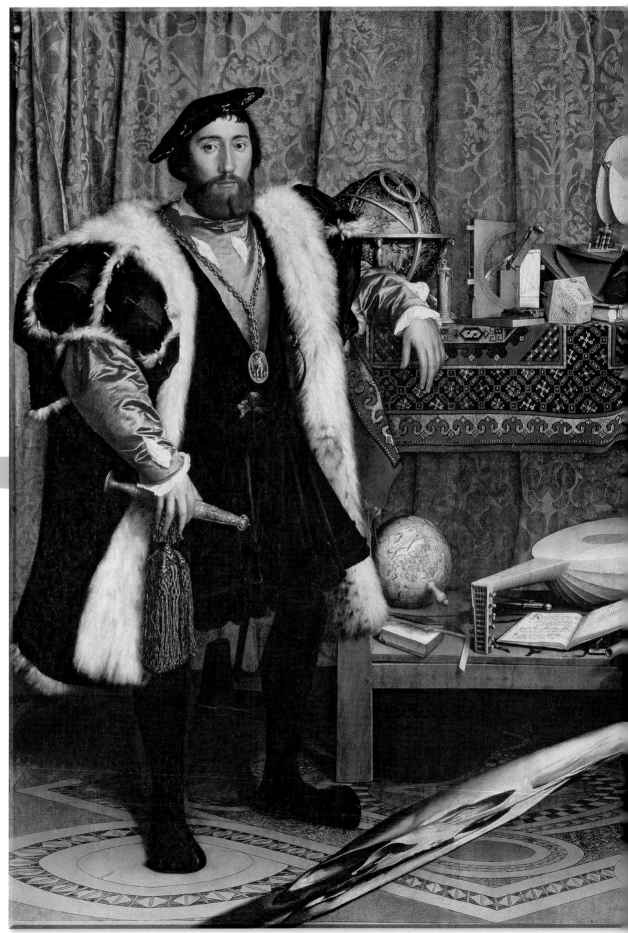

The Ambassadors

A political portrait

The Ambassadors, by the German artist Hans Holbein the Younger, is a life-size portrait of two Frenchmen who were sent to the court of English king Henry VIII to try to prevent war between the two rival countries. The rich fabrics of their clothing show that these are wealthy people, and the many objects that Holbein includes in the scene indicate that they are also educated. Each of these objects has its own meaning. The scientific instruments and globes refer to the developments in learning and exploration of the world, while the broken string on the musical instrument suggests the disharmony in the Church. When viewed from one side, the distorted shape at the bottom becomes a skull. It is not known why Holbein has included it here, but skulls in art are a symbol of mortality—a reminder that one day we will die.

Hans Holbein was called "the Younger" to distinguish him from **his father, Hans Holbein the Elder,** who was **also a celebrated painter** in Germany.

Persian miniature

Persian artist Mir Sayyid Ali was known for his lavish miniature paintings—a reputation that even took him to northern India, where he helped develop Mughal painting (see p.97). *Nighttime in a City* is typical of his style, teeming with fascinating stories and colorful characters.

Nighttime in a City

Faces are always shown in three-quarter profile.

Hands are always depicted with the thumb apart from the fingers.

1540

Persian miniatures were painted with thin brushes made from the fine tail hair of squirrels and cats.

The red rods identify the people as Safavids, a 16th-century dynasty of Persia.

The entire scene is shown on a flat plane with no use of perspective.

c. 1550–1599

Zen painting

The Chinese monks Hanshan and Shide were popular subjects in Zen Buddhist paintings from Japan. Shide (in front) was a caretaker in a Buddhist temple and Hanshan was a poet. Depictions of this mischievous, eccentric pair, such as this one by an unknown artist, usually showed them laughing together.

Hanshan and Shide

Mandalas
A mandala is a piece of art that helps people understand religious history or teachings. This 16th-century mandala shows Miroku Bosatsu, the founder of Japanese Hossō Buddhism, and the people who brought Buddhism from India and China to Japan.

Miroku Bosatsu sits on a lotus flower, a symbol of spiritual awakening.

The name of each person is inscribed next to them.

Hossō Mandala

Last Supper

1547

Protestant art

German artist Lucas Cranach the Elder supported the Protestant Reformation—a revolt against the Catholic Church. In his depiction of the Last Supper, Cranach includes the leading figure of the Reformation—Martin Luther (seated far right)— as one of Jesus's apostles. The cupbearer may be the artist himself.

1550

1560 ▶▶

A Meat Stall with the Holy Family Giving Alms

Crossed objects, such as these fish, represent the crucifix.

1551

Two pictures in one

Dutch artist Pieter Aertsen invented "inverted still lifes"—paintings in which a religious story or serious message forms the background of an impressive still life. Here, Aertsen shows Mary and Joseph giving alms to beggars in the distance behind a large meat stall.

1556

Self-portrait

Italian artist Sofonisba Anguissola is thought to be the first professional female painter of the Renaissance. She was also the first to combine a self-portrait at the easel with painting the Madonna and Child. Here, Anguissola is seen using a maulstick, held in her left hand, to keep her right hand steady as she paints.

Self-Portrait at the Easel Painting a Devotional Panel

The world turned upside down

This means that everything is the opposite of what it should be. By positioning a globe with a cross below it in a prominent place in the picture, Bruegel is pointing out that the Christian world is full of fools, as his scene shows!

Running like your backside is on fire

A farmer hurries to stop his crops being eaten while his backside is on fire. This refers to how foolish and pointless it is to run around because he is not going to escape the fire. A better solution would be to calm down and put out the fire, and then solve the problem.

To bell the cat

In one of Aesop's fables, a group of mice decide to put a bell around a cat's neck so they would know when the cat was coming. The failure of their plan is the origin of this proverb, meaning "to attempt an impossibly difficult task."

Banging your head against a brick wall

This signifies the frustration of being unable to alter some situations, no matter how hard you try. To keep on trying just adds to the pain and frustration!

Folktales and sayings
Netherlandish Proverbs, 1559, Pieter Bruegel the Elder

This oil-on-wood painting is a much-loved example of Dutch artist Pieter Bruegel's richly detailed and often humorous work. It appears at first to be just a bustling village scene, but a closer look reveals that Bruegel has cleverly depicted more than 100 proverbs (popular sayings), including some from *Aesop's Fables*—famous stories from ancient Greece. Although the proverbs are Dutch in origin, they are about situations that everyone has come across, and some of them offer wise advice.

Tossing feathers in the wind

This poor man is struggling to carry his basket of feathers on a windy day—a pointless task, as they are all flying away. This proverb cautions against starting a task without giving it much thought.

Big fish eat little fish

This grim scene carries a bleak message, that the strong tend to prey on the weak. A similar proverb, "there's always a bigger fish," suggests that however well you are doing in life, there is probably someone more successful than you.

Spilled porridge cannot be scraped up again

A man realizes that he is unable to scoop up his spilled porridge—meaning that once something is done, it cannot be undone. It is a reminder (like the similar saying "there's no use crying over spilled milk") that it is pointless to be upset about a past event, as it will not change the outcome.

Hunting party

Mirza 'Ali was a Persian artist who later moved to India, becoming a master of Mughal miniatures (see p.97). In this larger-scale painting from c.1570, a royal hunting party pauses for a rest.

The hawk used in the hunt is perched on the royal attendant's arm.

c. 1560

Realistic style

Caterina van Hemessen is the first female Flemish artist whose work has been identified. She was primarily a portrait painter and was known for her realism. In this portrait, she pays particular attention to the details of the headdress, lace collar, ruched sleeves, and metal buttons.

Portrait of a Young Lady

1560

Around 80 different flower species can be found in this painting.

c. 1563–1573

Quirky portrait

Italian painter Giuseppe Arcimboldo is best known for his imaginative and humorous portraits made from flowers, food, animals, and other objects. This work represents spring, and is part of a set of four called *The Four Seasons*. Arcimboldo worked for the German Hapsburg court, where the science of plants and animals were fields of great interest. This gave the artist access to a large collection of rare flora and fauna for his studies.

 The Hapsburg court allowed Arcimboldo to do more than just portrait painting. He also designed costumes and organized extravagant balls.

Spring

1520–1590 MANNERISM

In about 1520, a painting style called Mannerism emerged in Europe. Derived from the Italian word *maniera*, meaning "manner," it was both influenced by and a reaction to the Renaissance. Young artists felt they could not improve upon the techniques of Renaissance painters such as Leonardo da Vinci, and so tried new forms of expression, using elongated forms, odd spaces and settings, and unnatural colors.

Out of proportion
Painted by Italian artist Parmigianino in the late 1530s, *Madonna with the Long Neck* shows exaggerated proportions of both Mary and the baby Jesus, and a group of figures that is rather squeezed into the left side of the painting.

The Disrobing of Christ

1577–1579
El Greco's art
An artist from Crete known as El Greco, meaning "the Greek," got his nickname when he moved to Spain. He was a Mannerist, using dramatic action and lighting as well as bold colors, as in his depiction of Christ before the Crucifixion.

1570

1580 ▶▶

Gibbons in a Landscape

c. 1570
Painting wildlife
Gibbons, a species of ape, were a popular subject in Japanese art because of their mischievous nature. On this pair of screens, the artist, Zen Buddhist monk Sesson Shūkei, has illustrated the gibbons' futile task of trying to grab the reflection of the moon in the water below them. This refers to the Zen teaching of how easy it is to be fooled.

Mounted ruler

Late 1500s
King on horseback
The exact identity of the figure in this copper sculpture is unknown, but it is thought to be the King of Idah, who ruled over the Igala people in what is now central Nigeria. His feathered crown is a symbol of high rank, as is his coat covered with cowrie shells, which represented prosperity.

Russian folk art

A chalice veil is a cloth used to cover the chalice or cup of wine used in church services. In Russia, these were often intricately embroidered by country women as an evening pastime after their day's work.

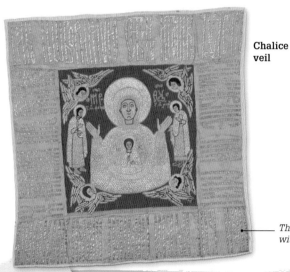

Pine trees

Chalice veil

Japanese ink painting

Sumi-e (ink painting) was considered to be one of the highest tests of an artist's skills, requiring expert control of the brush and the right balance of water and ink.

Late 1500s

Simple brushstrokes

Hasegawa Tohaku was a Japanese artist from the Azuchi-Momoyama period. This painting is an example of his *kotan* style, meaning "elegant simplicity." He used several brushes tied together, as well as a splintered bamboo stick, to make it look like a misty forest.

This example glistens with metallic thread.

1580

1590

1584–1585

Change of style

Paintings from the Baroque period (see pp.92–93) were often dramatic with elaborate decoration, but some artists also made quieter works based on everyday life. Many of Italian artist Annibale Carracci's paintings show grand scenes from the Bible or ancient mythology, but *The Bean Eater* is very different. It depicts an ordinary man eating a simple meal. Carracci changed from his usual Baroque style for this painting, using rough, broken brushwork that fits better with the country scene.

Still life has been skillfully combined with portraiture.

The Bean Eater

Young Sick Bacchus

1552–1614   LAVINIA FONTANA

Italian painter Lavinia Fontana made a living as an artist at a time when there were hardly any women painters. She was one of the most important Mannerist portrait painters in Bologna, Italy, and her husband, fellow artist Gian Paolo Zappi, acted as her assistant. He also took care of their 11 children while she worked, which was highly unusual for the time.

Family portrait
This is one of Fontana's finest portraits, showing Bianca degli Utili Maselli and 6 of her 19 children. It was painted in the early 1600s, and the artist has skillfully depicted details of the family's jewels, hairstyles, and the different textures of their expensive clothing.

1593–1594

Artist as a model
One of the first painters of the Baroque period (see pp.92–93), Italian artist Caravaggio is known for his dramatic use of *chiaroscuro*—the contrast of light and shade. In this early work, he has used a mirror to paint himself as the ancient Greco-Roman god of wine and festivity.

1600 ▶▶

Late 1500s

Ivory medallion
This ivory medallion was made in China and is about the size of an apple. The purpose of this object is unknown, but the intricately detailed three-dimensional carving perfectly showcases the artist's great skill. The scene shows a scholar and his assistants returning home by moonlight from a spring outing.

Elephants became extinct in China, partly due to the ivory trade. Ivory is now a banned substance to protect elephant populations around the world.

The lotus, peony, aster, and hibiscus blossoms show us that it is springtime.

Return From a Spring Outing

1600–1800

As the Renaissance gave way to the Baroque movement in Europe, art became more grand and dramatic. In Japan, the art of woodblock printing became popular and was used to create elaborate scenes from everyday life and folk tales. In the Indian subcontinent, art flourished under the Mughals, resulting in objects and buildings decorated with glittering gemstones, and lively paintings of myths and court life. By the 18th century, European artists were once again inspired to return to the Classical styles of ancient Greece and Rome.

Plant dyes, such as indigo, and pigments obtained from clays and charcoal were often used to add color to fabrics.

Tunic from West Africa

1600s

Royal robes

Textiles are a very important part of African cultures and traditions, with distinctive patterns and motifs that reflect Africa's rich history. In west central Africa, textiles were a symbol of wealth, collected by royals and other important people—and often traded with other countries. This royal tunic from the Kingdom of Ardra (in modern-day Benin) was exported to Europe in the mid-17th century.

1600–1750   BAROQUE ART

In the 17th century, a new art movement called Baroque emerged—focusing on drama, movement, and realism using rich, deep colors. While Renaissance paintings had aimed to show carefully balanced proportions (see p.79), Baroque art set out to appeal to the viewer's senses and emotion. Originating in Italy, it soon spread across Europe and was particularly popular with the Catholic Church.

In the beast's lair

In *Daniel In the Lion's Den* (c. 1614–1616), Dutch artist Peter Paul Rubens has used dramatic lighting along with Daniel's heightened emotions to grab the viewer's attention. The snarling lions look lifelike, giving the viewer a sense of the danger.

1600

1615

The Gods of Wind and Thunder

The painting was made into a pair of folding screens.

1615

Doves and dragons

In this illustrated manuscript, Armenian artist Mesrop of Khizan depicts Jesus's baptism in a unique way. Along with the dove, which in Western art represents the Holy Spirit, he shows Jesus standing on a *vishap*—an Armenian dragon that symbolizes water, wealth, and power.

Early 1600s

Natural forces

Two Shinto deities, Raijin the god of thunder and lightning (left) and Fujin the wind god (right), face off against each other in this painting by Japanese artist Tawaraya Sōtatsu. Using ink and color on gold-leaf paper, the artist uses bold, wide strokes that highlight the gods' outlines and fierce expressions. A mix of silver paint and black ink gives the effect of stormy clouds as the gods float in the air.

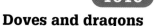

The Baptism of Christ

Slaying a giant

Italian sculptor Gian Lorenzo Bernini's *David* (1623–1624) brilliantly captures the movement and mental tension of the hero, as he gathers his strength and courage to attack the giant Goliath. The emotion and concentration on the statue's face really bring him to life.

A shocking revelation

In *Supper at Emmaus* (1601), sharply contrasting light and shadows, together with exaggerated gestures, help Italian artist Caravaggio to capture the dramatic moment when the newly resurrected Jesus reveals himself to two of his unsuspecting disciples.

Caravaggio uses the technique of foreshortening (see p.79) to give the illusion of the hand dramatically projecting into space.

1630

Early 1600s

Poetry recital

These ceramic tiles from Persia (modern-day Iran) depict a picnic in a lush garden, with a pair of figures reciting poetry to one another (center). The artist has used water-based glazes to paint the tiles. The glazes are separated by a waxy substance to prevent their colors from mixing when the tiles are fired in a kiln. This produces sharp lines and bright, clean colors.

The man is writing in a poetry book called a safina.

The colorful, patterned robes and silk sashes are typical of outfits depicted in 17th-century Persian art.

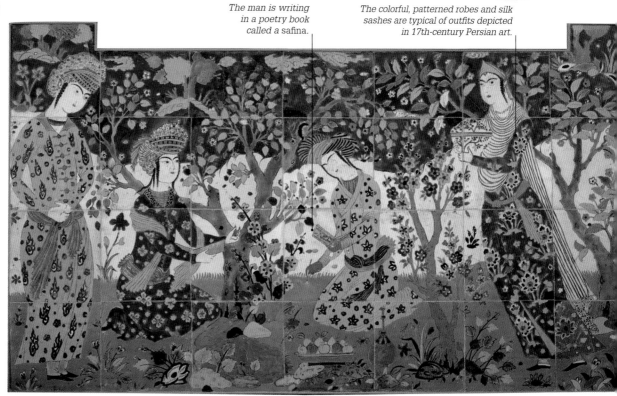

Reciting Poetry in a Garden

Hunting for demons

The 17th-century Chinese artist Zheng Zhong is known for his paintings of landscapes and Buddhist themes. Zheng's *Searching the Mountains for Demons*, a 27-ft- (8-m-) wide handscroll painting that is read from right to left, depicts the legend of Erlang, the Chinese demigod who is responsible for controlling floods. The painting follows the warrior hero and his army as they chase after troops of wild animals and demons, as well as a fierce dragon that has caused a flood. In this scene, Erlang sits under a tree, holding his famous dragon-slaying double-edged sword while his assistants give him news. Other demon-slayers, identifiable by their clawed feet, stand nearby.

Section of *Searching the Mountains for Demons*

Erlang's perilous adventure unfolds
over many scenes in **one continuous
scroll**—a classic example of the
Chinese art of storytelling.

1630 ▶ 1660

The Infant Moses Trampling Pharaoh's Crown

c. 1634

Literary painting

Tawaraya Sōtatsu was one of the founders of the Rimpa school of Japanese art, which paired poetry with paintings. In his illustration of an episode from the 10th-century *Tales of Ise*, the poem (top right) highlights the events unfolding in the scene.

Mount Utsu from *Tales of Ise*

c. 1645–1646

Going against tradition

French artist Nicolas Poussin often chose unusual subjects or themes for his paintings. In this work he provides a different take on the Biblical story of Moses. The scene shows the infant Moses trampling the Pharaoh's crown to the shock of bystanders, signaling that he would one day overthrow the Pharaoh.

1659

Painting a princess

Infanta Margarita in a Blue Dress

Using a palette of dense blue, gold, and silver, Spanish court artist Diego Velázquez conveys the fine clothing of Princess Margarita, the eight-year-old daughter of Mariana and King Philip IV of Spain. This portrait was sent to her future husband to show him what she looked like.

1630 ——————————————— **1660**

1642

Dutch masterpiece

Dutch artist Rembrandt was known for his expressive paintings. One of his most well-known works, *The Night Watch*, shows a patrol by Amsterdam's civic guards, who defended the city. The artist expertly uses the light to focus on the most important figures in the composition—including the young girl, the guards' mascot.

1593–1653 ARTEMISIA GENTILESCHI

Italian artist Artemisia Gentileschi is one of the most celebrated female painters of the 17th century. At a time when women were not encouraged to follow artistic pursuits, Gentileschi became the first female member of the Academy of the Arts of Drawing in Florence, Italy. Her work is typical of the Baroque style (see pp.92–93).

Self-portrait

In *Self-Portrait as the Allegory of Painting* (1638–1639), Gentileschi combines two elements: a self-portrait and a representation of a "female painter," which was extremely rare at the time. The artist is boldly promoting herself as the perfect example of what it means to be a painter.

The Night Watch

1580–1650   MUGHAL ART

The Mughal Empire ruled the Indian subcontinent for more than 300 years, between 1526 and 1857. At the peak of their rule, in the 16th century, Mughal courts became well known for housing artists from different cultural and religious traditions. It was during this time that a unique artistic style grew out of a combination of Hindu, Persian, and even European painting and decorative traditions, creating a wealth of Mughal art that included paintings, craftwork, ornaments, and architecture.

Decorated flask

This 17th-century horn-shaped flask was designed to hold gunpowder. It is made of wood, unlike other similar vessels, which were made of ivory. The flask is decorated with a blue-and-black lacquer coating and elaborate gold floral designs typical of Mughal art.

Miniature paintings

Mughal artists were best known for their miniatures. They would create these small illustrations for books or for a *muraqqa*, an album combining paintings with calligraphy. During Emperor Shah Jahan's reign, miniatures usually took on the form of portraits and courtly scenes, such as this one made in 1630, where the emperor can be seen accepting a falcon as a gift.

Swirling blue-and-black patterns provide a deep background for the gold decoration.

This intricately designed hilt is embedded with emeralds and rubies.

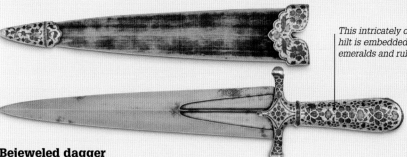

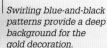

Bejeweled dagger

This dagger and scabbard (cover) were probably made during the reign of Mughal emperor Jahangir (1605–1627). He was known to love flowers, and the floral design is typical of the art made during his reign. The decorative parts are made of gold and set with precious stones and colored glass.

Inlaid marble

Flowers were a popular motif in Mughal art, because they reflected the Islamic idea of paradise as a beautiful garden. Mughal craftspeople inlaid marble with gemstones in a style called *parchin kari*, using it to decorate their buildings. The most famous example is the Taj Mahal, which houses the panel shown here.

1660 ▸ 1680

The Art of Painting

Painting a painter

Dutch painter Johannes Vermeer is known for his scenes of calm interiors, with people illuminated by soft light from a window. In *The Art of Painting*, he depicts the artist at work in a beautifully decorated room as opposed to a messy studio, presenting an idealized view of what it means to be a painter.

The curtain tricks the viewer into thinking they are entering the room.

> **"He created a world more perfect than any he had witnessed."**
>
> Art historian Walter Liedtke on Vermeer

1660

TROMPE L'OEIL

The French term *trompe l'oeil* means "trick the eye," and describes art that is so realistic that it makes the viewer wonder if they are looking at the real thing rather than a depiction. The technique began in ancient Greece, but gained popularity during the Renaissance, reaching its peak with 17th-century Flemish and Dutch painters. These master illusionists loved subjects such as peeling paper, people tapping at windows, and fruit that looked good enough to eat.

Just an illusion

In *Trompe l'oeil Studio Wall with a Vanitas Still Life* (1664), Flemish artist Cornelis Norbertus Gijsbrechts creates the illusion of the canvas coming loose from the frame. The work is an example of "Vanitas" art, which uses objects like skulls to symbolize the certainty of death.

Out of the frame

Catalan painter Pere Borrell del Caso's *Escaping Criticism* (1874) is his most famous work and is a classic example of *trompe l'oeil*. In his eagerness to avoid a telling-off, the boy looks as if he is climbing out of the picture frame.

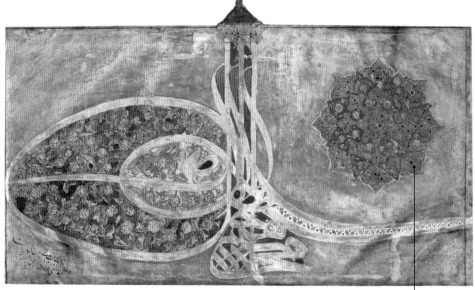

Tughra of Ottoman Sultan Mehmed IV

The flower in turquoise and gold adds another decorative element to the royal signature.

Late 1600s

Turkish calligraphy

Turkish calligraphers would make their own pens, inks, and paper. They created a unique art form where words were transformed into patterns using rich colors. Examples of this calligraphy were *tughra*—calligraphic seals or signatures of the sultans of the Ottoman Empire (centered in modern-day Turkey) that incorporated the sultan's name as well as other symbols of the empire (highlighted here in gold).

Inca vessel

This 17th-century cup, called a *kero*, may have been used by the Inca people of South America to drink *chicha*—a beer made from corn—during social gatherings. It shows people wearing both Inca and Western clothing.

Plants and large cats are painted around the bottom.

1670

1672

1680

Lively classroom

Dutch artist Jan Steen painted bustling scenes from everyday life. He was known for his mischievous sense of humor and his skill at storytelling through art. In this painting, children wreak havoc—fighting, destroying books, and jumping on furniture—right under the nose of a sleeping teacher.

This boy is standing on his desk, happily singing.

Jan Steen's chaotic paintings inspired the Dutch saying "a Jan Steen household," meaning "a messy house."

A Riotous Schoolroom with a Snoozing Schoolmaster

A temple visit

This arched wooden bridge leads across the river to a *sekiya* (barrier gate), the entrance to a Buddhist temple. Genji has stepped down from his carriage and is making his way there. Here and elsewhere, trees are used to separate the different episodes in Genji's story.

A game of soccer

In a famous scene from the *Tale*, Kashiwagi— Genji's rival—is playing *kemari* (a type of soccer) with his courtiers. When a cat runs out from behind a screen, Kashiwagi catches a glimpse of Genji's wife, the Third Princess, and falls in love with her.

A springtime story

Scenes from the Tale of Genji, 1677, Kanō Tsunenobu

The *Tale of Genji* is a classic of Japanese literature, written in the 11th century by Murasaki Shikibu, a poet and lady-in-waiting at the Imperial Court. The novel recounts the adventures at court of its hero, Prince Genji, and was a common subject for vibrantly colorful screen paintings such as this one, created by Tsunenobu, an artist of the Kanō school—the dominant style in Japanese art from the 15th to the 19th centuries. The 12 scenes depicted can be viewed in any order.

Spring blossom

Cherry blossom (*sakura*) holds a special place in Japanese art and culture. It symbolizes hope and renewal, but as it lasts for just two weeks, it also emphasizes that life is short—a reminder to stop and appreciate the moment.

Genji stages a concert

In this scene, Genji has arranged for female musicians at court to perform a concert for the emperor. Two women play the *koto*, a long, plucked instrument—the national instrument of Japan.

Open roof

The artist uses a device called *fukinuki yatai* ("blown-off roof") to give viewers a look inside the buildings. The interior walls contain detailed monochrome landscapes—a contrast to the colorful depictions of the main action.

1680 ▸ 1700

🔈 The *Simurgh*, which means "30 birds" in Persian, refers to a phoenixlike mythical creature that symbolizes the union of heaven and earth in Sufi poetry.

Anthology of Persian Poetry

The flowering tree indicates springtime.

c. 1680s
Safavid art
Falconers hunting in springtime is a common theme in Islamic art. Here, a falconer can be seen sitting in a flowering tree with a Persian mythical bird called a *simurgh* flying above. This illustration, which was made on paper sprinkled with gold, forms part of a *safina*, meaning "boat," which is a long, narrow book of works by the poets of the Safavid Dynasty of Persia (modern-day Iran).

c. 1690
Indian miniatures
Basohli painting is a miniature style from the Himalayan states of India. These paintings have distinctive red borders and use vibrant colors. An unknown artist captures a moment of personal devotion in this example by showing a blind *maharaja* (king) in meditation.

Maharaja Sital Dev in Devotion

 1680 ● ○ **1690**

c. 1681
Inventive painter
English portrait painter Mary Beale studied different techniques and even painted on unusual materials, such as sacks and onion bags. In *Portrait of a Young Girl*, she experimented with painting in a single session, producing a work that feels free and informal.

Portrait of a Young Girl

c. 1690
Early Japanese woodblock print
Japanese artist Sugimura Jihei was known to portray deep emotion in his woodblock prints. This example focuses on the folk hero Kumagai Renshobo, who became a monk in remorse for killing a 15-year-old warrior named Taira no Atsumori in battle. The artist depicts Renshobo imagining Taira still alive and with his parents.

The Vision of Kumagai Renshobo

JAPANESE WOODBLOCK PRINTING

Woodblock printing was imported from China and became popular in Japan during the Edo period (1603–1867). Initially used for Buddhist scriptures, woodblock prints were soon used by artists to depict everyday scenes and stories in a style known as *ukiyo-e* ("pictures of the floating world"). Making the print required several different artisans.

Chisels

Carving a scene
First, the artist made a drawing on semi-transparent paper. A woodcarver placed the paper onto a block of wood, and chiseled out the design so that the lines stood out, as seen here. The printer then applied watercolor or ink to the block.

Finished print
The painted block was pressed onto paper to transfer the design. The block could only be painted with one color, so multicolored scenes, such as *Enjoying the Evening Cool* (1906) by Yamamoto Shoun, needed a separate block for each pigment.

1700

Late 1600s

Ethiopian triptych
A triptych is a painting with three panels that is used for religious rituals. This Christian triptych from Ethiopia shows Mary and the infant Jesus in the center, surrounded by the apostles, while the other two panels depict stories from the Bible. The figures have the large, expressive eyes that were a distinctive feature of Ethiopian Christian art at this time.

Triptych Center Panel with Mary and Her Son and Christ Teaching the Apostles

Tiny dots of paint are used to create different patterns on the robes.

A panel painting was believed to actually represent the holy person it portrayed.

Krishna's kindness

Krishna Lifts Mount Govardhan, c. 1690, Sahībdīn

A much-loved tale from Hindu mythology tells the story of Krishna, the human form of God Vishnu, and Indra, the god of rain. When Krishna discovers that the people living next to Mount Govardhan are worshipping Indra, he asks them to stop. As punishment, furious Indra whips up a terrifying storm to flood their village. Krishna, known for his kindness, lifts up the mountain to shelter and protect the people and their cows. Indian artist Sahībdīn uses gouache on paper to produce the muted colors seen here. This technique is characteristic of India's Bikaner school of painting, which was heavily influenced by Mughal art.

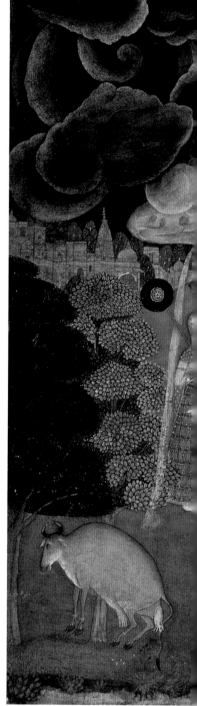

Krishna, the protector
Calm and perfectly at ease, Krishna stands at the center, supporting the mountain with one finger, while holding his flute in the other hand. He holds up the mountain for a week without moving, using his divine strength.

Light and shade
The darkest part of the painting is the rain clouds rolling across the sky. Light from the mountain picks out the details of the trees, with a combination of light and dark shades highlighting each leaf. Just visible in the background is the village.

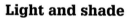

Krishna's followers
The women offer Krishna their thanks and present him with gifts. Each woman is a *gopi*—a milkmaid who has fallen in love with Krishna. Their faces show a lack of any fear, even of the storm, highlighting their faith in and devotion to their protector.

Mount Govardhan
Green areas between rocky ridges show that the mountain is an ideal spot for grazing cows. The name of the mountain translates as *Go* for "cow" and *Vardhan* for "nourishment."

A stormy arrival
The rain god Indra (front) is seen among the storm clouds he created, accompanied by a servant and riding on Airavata, his elephant. Airavata's legs are hidden by the swirling mass of dark clouds around it.

1700 ▶ 1730

1703

Dramatic portrait

French artist Nicolas de Largillière is known for his dramatic portraits, and this painting is considered one of his finest works. Although the identity of the woman is unknown, her clothing is typical of the aristocracy of the city of Strasbourg at the time. Largillière shows off her delicate complexion and white lace, which stand out against her black clothing and hat.

The Beautiful Strasbourg Woman

1700

Qing jade figurines

These 18th-century jade figurines of two serving boys are typical of the carvings made in the emperor's workshops during China's Qing period. Probably made as a set, they were rediscovered separately, 80 years apart!

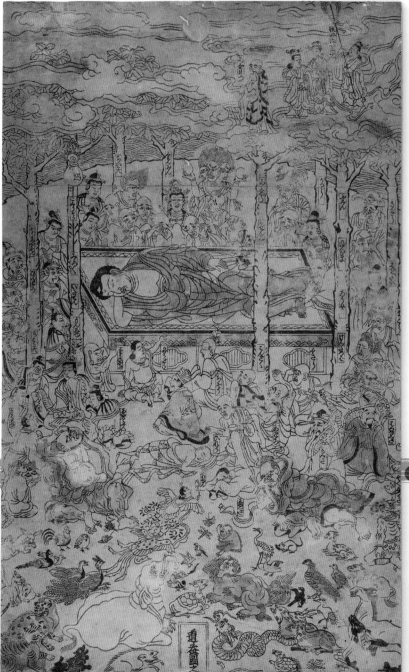

Death of the Buddha

1711–1714

Gaining enlightenment

The death of the Buddha is a popular theme in Buddhist art because it presents the ultimate goal—passing from earthly life to become an enlightened being. In this woodblock painting by Japanese artist Doeki, the Buddha is shown as the largest figure to symbolize his greatness. Everyone else mourns his death, including the animals in the foreground.

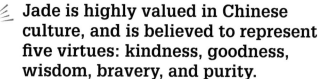 Jade is highly valued in Chinese culture, and is believed to represent five virtues: kindness, goodness, wisdom, bravery, and purity.

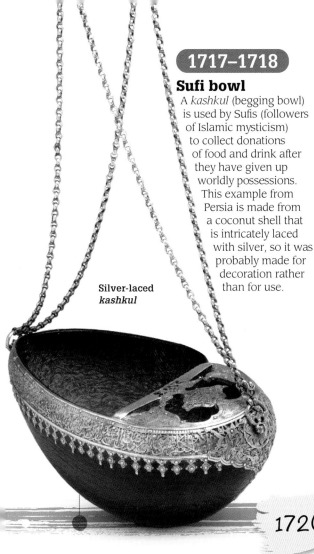

1717–1718
Sufi bowl
A *kashkul* (begging bowl) is used by Sufis (followers of Islamic mysticism) to collect donations of food and drink after they have given up worldly possessions. This example from Persia is made from a coconut shell that is intricately laced with silver, so it was probably made for decoration rather than for use.

Silver-laced
kashkul

1647–1717   MARIA SIBYLLA MERIAN

Swiss illustrator Maria Sibylla Merian was fascinated with plants and animals from a young age, eventually becoming one of the most talented botanical artists of her time. She even traveled to South America, where she painted interesting animals and insects.

Watercolor wonder
In the early 1700s, during her trip to Suriname, Merian made this watercolor illustration of a spectacled caiman trying to protect its egg from a false coral snake.

1720

1730 ▶▶

c. 1725
Lion-hunter
The Kota school of painting from Rajasthan, India, is known for its vivid royal hunting scenes. Here, a great warrior-king (bottom left) gets ready to attack gigantic lions in the middle of a forest. The artist uses fine lines and pale colors to define the forms of the animals, and gives them monstrous faces. The king's hunting group is wonderfully camouflaged in the undergrowth.

Rao Raja Bhoj Singh of Bundi Slays a Lion

1730 ▶ 1760

The Graham Children

c. 1733–1734
Blowing bubbles
French artist Jean-Siméon Chardin loved to paint scenes from everyday life, such as this one of a boy blowing a bubble while a younger child watches on. In art, bubbles are a symbol for the fact that life passes quickly—these boys will not stay young for long.

Cherries were considered the fruit of paradise, showing that baby Thomas had gone to heaven.

Soap Bubbles

1742
Family memento
At first glance, this painting by expert English portrait artist William Hogarth looks like a happy family scene, with the smiling children of Royal Apothecary (pharmacist) Daniel Graham surrounded by their pets. In reality, the youngest child, Thomas, had already died, so the portrait was made as a way of remembering him.

1730

The Grand Canal

Recording images
A camera obscura is a type of camera that captures an image of a scene upside down on an inside surface. This image could be used by artists to ensure their measurements and perspectives were correct.

1730s
Canaletto's Venice
Italian artist Canaletto painted his home city of Venice many times. His paintings were so realistic that tourists would take them home as a reminder of their visit. Canaletto probably used a camera obscura (see right) to create accurate images that could be traced for the painting, with the details of the bustling waterways added in freehand.

1744

Bird's-eye view

During this action-packed hunt, a hawk catches a crane for a *maharana* (king). An aerial perspective (view from above) shows the story unfold in a series of scenes over a large canvas. This is typical of Mewar painting from Rajasthan, India, which combined Indigenous artistic traditions with Mughal styles (see p.97).

Laila and Majnun

The hunt begins here with the release of a hunting hawk.

Maharana Jagat Singh Hawks for Cranes

c. 1750s

Persian oil painting

Around this time, oil painting was introduced to Persia (modern-day Iran). Here, the famous Persian lovers Laila (left) and Majnun (right) are placed in three-quarter view, typical of Persian art of the time. The artist also creates depth in the scene, similar to contemporary works from Europe.

1745

1760 ▶▶

Late 1700s

Supernatural portrait

Japanese artist Maruyama Okyo was fascinated by ghosts, and developed the *yurei-zu* ("faint spirit") school of painting, which specialized in supernatural themes. In *The Ghost of Oyuki*, the artist has painted his dead lover Oyuki with the messy hair and white robes usually associated with ghosts.

The Ghost of Oyuki

1730–1770   ROCOCO PERIOD

Toward the end of the Baroque era, a movement called Rococo emerged among French artists who were tired of the formal style promoted by King Louis XIV. Highly theatrical and ornamental, it was characterized by soft colors and flowing, natural lines, and typically focused on lighthearted themes such as people having fun in the countryside.

Pastoral scenes

French painter François Boucher's *Lovers in a Park* (1758) is typical of the idealized outdoor scenes favored by Rococo artists.

Pastel palette

Rococo artists preferred pastel colors, moving away from the deep tones of the Baroque style. Designs were often inspired by nature and had irregular patterns, as shown by this English-made porcelain candleholder from c. 1765.

Gilding added the final touches to the ornamental Rococo style.

Medieval selfie, 1170–1200

Brother Rufillus, a German monk, has made sure everyone knows who decorated this colorful medieval manuscript. He depicts himself painting an "R" for "Rufillus," surrounded by paint pots. At the time, there was no machinery to print books, and it was left to monks and nuns—who were among the only people able to read and write—to copy out and illustrate texts by hand.

Self Portrait at the Age of 34   *Self Portrait at the Age of 63*

The passing of time, 1630 and 1669

Dutch painter Rembrandt used himself as a subject to experiment with different light and techniques. His portrait at age 34 suggests wealth and confidence. By age 63, his face is worn and softened by wrinkles.

Almost lifelike, 1500

Self-Portrait with Fur-Trimmed Robe by German artist Albrecht Dürer is remarkable for the realistic detail of his skin, hair, and clothing. The penetrating gaze, straight at the viewer, was very unusual for its time.

A portrait in needlework, 1779

This self-portrait is embroidered from wool. It shows the English artist Mary Knowles stitching a "needle painting" of King George III. Her work is so skillfully finished, using fine wools in subtly varying colors, that it has the softness of a painting.

Self-portraits

The 21st century may be the age of the selfie, but artists have been portraying themselves for thousands of years. Few examples from ancient times survive, but from the medieval era onward, self-portraits became an increasingly important branch of art. Some artists focus on creating an accurate picture of themselves, whereas others are more interested in expressing their personality—often using innovative techniques.

Mysterious symbols, 1889
This colorful self-portrait by French artist Paul Gauguin is both eye-catching and mysterious. He shows just his head and hand, together with the Christian symbols of a halo, apples, and a snake. They seem like clues, perhaps suggesting different aspects of his personality.

Digital sculpture, 2017
British artist Jonathan Yeo used virtual reality painting tools and 3D printing to create *Homage to Paolozzi (Self Portrait)*: a sculpture of his head, cast from the printed model. Its title refers to the influential British artist, Eduardo Paolozzi, in whose former studio Yeo is based.

Overlapping bronze plates re-create the artist's virtual brushstrokes.

Mixing materials, 2016
Wedding Souvenirs depicts Nigerian-American artist Njideka Akunyili Crosby before a mirror, surrounded by reminders of her wedding (and that of her brother). She uses collage, mixing paint, pencils, and traditional Nigerian cloth to reflect the various experiences, people, and places that have made her who she is.

111

Lion and Dragon in Combat

Late 1700s

Fighting beasts

Persian artist Muhammad Baqir depicts a lion and a dragon in combat. This is an unusual pairing, because these two powerful creatures are traditionally shown defeating weaker ones. Who knows which will win, but the artist has used a little bit of red in this ink and watercolor painting to show that the lion is the first to draw blood.

Lacquered case

Small wooden boxes, called *inrō*, were used in Japan to carry medicines and small items. This late 18th-century lacquered *inrō* was made by Japanese artist Koami Nagataka. It has silken cords and an ivory bead that secure its contents.

The little ivory dog is known as a netsuke (carved miniature).

Dragonfly motif

1760

c. 1766

Woodblock print

Japanese artist Suzuki Harunobu was the first to create multi-colored woodblock prints in the *ukiyo-e* style (see p.103). His works show peaceful scenes from home life. Here, two women prepare to play a musical instrument called the *koto*. A branch of bush clover behind the screen shows it is fall.

The bridges (devices that support the strings) of the koto appear in a row, much like geese descending from the sky, which gives this artwork its name.

Descending Geese of the Koto Bridges

1769

A fashionable sport

English artist Joshua Reynolds's life-size portrait shows two aristocratic young men dressed as medieval archers. The work celebrates the men's friendship through the sport of archery, which became fashionable during this period among the upper classes. It was a sign of their high status in the world.

Colonel Acland and Lord Sydney: The Archers

1770

Bundi art

Miniature paintings from the Bundi district of Rajasthan, India, were known for their vibrant depictions of tales from Hindu mythology and the daily lives of the royalty. In this painting, the artist has created distinctive clothes and jewelery for each figure. Their faces, placed in profile, reveal the influence of Mughal art (see p.97).

A raja on horseback with attendants

1727–1788   THOMAS GAINSBOROUGH

British artist Thomas Gainsborough spent his childhood sketching in the fields and woods around his home in Suffolk, England. He grew to become an influential artist, and gained fame as one of Britain's greatest portrait painters. While his portraits were much sought-after, Gainsborough preferred painting landscapes and became the first artist to combine the two styles by placing his portrait subjects in outdoor scenes.

Famous portrait, 1770
One of Gainsborough's most famous portraits gained the nickname *The Blue Boy* due to its subject's vibrant blue satin clothes. The young boy seems both shy and serious.

770 ——————————————— **1780** ▶▶

The Academicians of the Royal Academy

1771–1772

Origins of the Royal Academy

This painting by German artist Johan Zoffany shows all the founding members of the Royal Academy of Arts, which was the first society for artists in England. The painting is infamous for featuring only the male founders as figures and placing the two female founders—Angelica Kauffman and Mary Moser—as portraits on the wall (top right).

Angelica Kauffman

Swiss Neoclassical artist Angelica Kauffman was one of the most important painters of her time. Kauffman learned to paint at a very young age, and came to be well known for her portraits and history paintings later in life.

Candlelight experiments

An Experiment on a Bird in the Air Pump, 1768, Joseph Wright of Derby

The British artist known as Joseph Wright of Derby lived during an era of major scientific developments. At the time, it was popular for scientists to travel around the country with their equipment, and demonstrate experiments in people's homes—something that was both educational and entertaining. In this dramatic scene, lit by a single candle, Wright brilliantly captures the different reactions of the audience during one such experiment, providing a glimpse into this fascinating period of history.

Couple in love

While everyone else is absorbed in the experiment, this young couple are caught gazing at each other. Wright has placed the pair in a shadowy corner of the scene, as if to emphasize this private moment.

Full moon

The full moon is a reference to the Lunar Society. This group of learned men met on nights with a full moon to discuss scientific topics. With no streetlamps to guide their way, the moonlight allowed them to get home safely.

The experiment

The main figure, a traveling scientist, demonstrates how an air pump works. As all the air is sucked out of the container to create a vacuum, the bird appears to take its last gasp. The figure looks out of the painting, as if he is asking the viewer to pay attention.

Worried children

The dramatic lighting draws attention to the two children and their distress at the fate of the bird, which is emphasized by the little girl grabbing hold of the older one's dress. The man behind them is perhaps explaining what is going on in the experiment.

Glass on the table

What lies at the bottom of the glass? It might be the lungs of a dead animal, which were often used in the air pump experiment instead of a bird. It could also be a skull, signifying how every living thing dies.

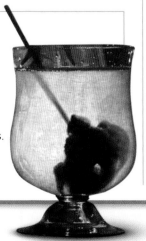

1780 ▶ 1800

🗣 George Stubbs also painted lions and giraffes, which he had seen in the private menageries (animal collections) of wealthy Europeans.

A Bay Hunter, a Springer Spaniel, and a Sussex Spaniel

Art meets science

To create his highly accurate paintings of horses, George Stubbs dissected dead horses layer by layer, sketching what he saw. These detailed drawings are found in his book *The Anatomy of the Horse* (1766).

1782

Stubbs' horses

British artist George Stubbs is best known for his paintings of animals—in particular, horses. He largely taught himself to paint and, because his depictions were so accurate, he was much in demand among wealthy owners as an animal portrait painter.

1780

1760–1860   NEOCLASSICISM

The rediscovery of the buried ancient Roman city of Pompeii, Italy, in the 1700s renewed interest in the art and architecture of the Classical world. The romanticized Rococo style (see p.109) gave way to the precision and simplicity of the movement called Neoclassicism. Artists used clearly defined forms, straight lines, and smooth finishes with no indication of brushstrokes.

Symbolic art
French artist Jacques-Louis David took well-known stories and painted them with a different message. In *Oath of the Horatii* (1784), he paints an ancient Roman tale of a family who swear to defend their city against their enemy. After the French Revolution, this painting came to symbolize the sacrifices people make for their country.

Kabuki Actor Ōtani Oniji III as Yakko Edobei

📢 Not much is known about Tōshūsai Sharaku, except that he made more than 140 woodblock portraits over the course of 10 months, before mysteriously disappearing.

1794
Painting an actor
Kabuki is a type of Japanese drama that uses exaggerated acting and elaborate makeup. This woodblock painting of a *kabuki* actor was made by Japanese artist Tōshūsai Sharaku. The artist has skillfully captured the actor's dramatic expressions as he plays the wicked character of Yakko Edobei.

Colorful bag
This impressive shoulder bag was made by a female artist from the Indigenous Ojibwe people of North America. It uses colorful beads for the strap, and dyed porcupine quills for the mazelike panels and the zigzag motifs at the edges.

The tassels are made of deer hair and wool.

1790

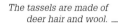

1800 ▶▶

c. 1795
Dreamy cityscape
British artist Thomas Girtin was an extremely talented watercolorist. He traveled around Britain painting landscapes and developing his unique style, beginning with accurate representations, before becoming more abstract over time. This painting of a busy London street shows a combination of great detail and loose, romantic brushwork.

St. Paul's Cathedral from St. Martin's-le-Grand

Neoclassical sculpture
Danish artist Bertel Thorvaldsen was one of the leading Neoclassical sculptors of his time. For *Ganymede and the Eagle* (1817–1829), he takes his subject from Greek mythology, depicting the young prince Ganymede naked, reflecting the ancient Greek and Roman belief that the human body was a beautiful and perfect form.

The Greek god Zeus is disguised as an eagle.

Watercolors
Watercolor paint uses pigments that dissolve in water. Thin layers of delicate color can be built up, but they are transparent, reflecting the paper beneath to give a luminous effect.

117 ▶

1800–1900

The 19th century was a time of technological change. In Europe and the US, objects could now be mass-produced, leaving some to wonder if craft skills would be lost forever. New printing techniques led to more accessible forms of art, such as posters and book illustration. As the world opened up to more travel and trade, European artists were influenced by Japanese woodcut prints and African sculptures. The invention of photography meant that art no longer needed to represent things realistically. Artists instead became fascinated with colors and shapes—a trend that continued well into the 20th century.

1800 ▸ 1820

Lion Dance of the New Year

c. 1800–1850
African tie-dye
This striking piece of cloth is from The Gambia, West Africa. Artists created its starburst pattern by loosely tying strings around sections of the cloth and then dunking it into a bath of indigo dye.

West African tie-dye textile

c. 1800–1806
New Year scene
Japanese artist Kitagawa Utamaro created woodblock prints in the *ukiyo-e* style (meaning "pictures of the floating world"). *Ukiyo-e* showed brightly colored and entertaining scenes of city life, as seen in this picture of a New Year celebration.

1800

1800

Painting royalty
Charles IV of Spain and His Family is a royal portrait by the Spanish painter Francisco Goya. Appointed first court painter in 1799, Goya here paints the Spanish royal family in expensive clothes and jewels. Only a few years later, Napoleon conquered Spain, taking away the family's wealth and power.

Charles IV of Spain and His Family

NAPOLEON'S IMAGE-MAKER

Napoleon Bonaparte was the ruler of France in the early 19th century. He was very ambitious, waging battle with many countries in his quest for power. In 1804, he appointed the French artist Jacques-Louis David as his official painter. Napoleon liked how David's Neoclassical style portrayed him as grand and heroic, connecting him to the great achievements of ancient Greece and Rome.

On the Alps
David's *Napoleon Crossing the Alps* (1801–1805) commemorates Napoleon's victory over the Austrians. In the bottom left-hand corner, "Bonaparte" is carved alongside the names Hannibal and Charlemagne, two powerful leaders whose troops had also crossed the Alps.

US Capitol
Many public buildings in Europe and the US, such as the US Capitol, are built in Neoclassical style. Begun in 1793, the Capitol's grand scale but simple, symmetrical structure reflects the buildings of ancient Greece and Rome.

The angled head shows the dancer's movement.

Dancer with Cymbals

1809
Capitol columns
In ancient Greece and Rome, the capital (top part) of a column usually had acanthus leaf decorations. US architect Benjamin Henry Latrobe wanted something distinctly American for the US Capitol building, so he replaced the acanthus leaves with ears of corn—a widely grown crop.

Column at the US Capitol

1811–1812
Lifelike figure
Just like the ancient Greeks and Romans, Italian sculptor Antonio Canova carved marble into lifelike figures such as this one of a dancer. He captures a sense of movement by putting her on her tiptoes, as if to show that she is in the middle of a dance.

1810

1820

The Wanderer above the Sea of Fog

c. 1818
In awe of nature
The Wanderer above the Sea of Fog by German artist Caspar David Friedrich depicts the awe-inspiring beauty and power of nature. The vast landscape stretches out before the man, showing him to be tiny and insignificant in the face of its forces.

121

Dance in art

Dance presents artists with a seemingly impossible challenge: how to capture movement and emotion using materials such as bronze and paint. Throughout history and across cultures, artists have often used similar devices to convey the steps of a dance: a raised foot, outstretched arms, or flowing clothing or hair. The best-loved artwork shows how dance is a way for people to express themselves and truly live in the moment.

Lord of Dance, c. 1000s

This form of the Hindu God Shiva, called Nataraja or the "Lord of Dance," was the main deity worshipped during the Chola Dynasty in India. This bronze icon depicts him performing the *tandava*, a cosmic dance which signaled the creation or destruction of the universe. Surrounded by a ring of fire, he maintains perfect balance on one leg, representing his role in holding the universe in balance.

Dance of joy, c. 25–220 CE

Animated earthenware figures like this one have been found in Han Dynasty tombs in China. The sculptor was more interested in capturing the dancer's mood than creating a realistic portrait. The figure's wide smile and stance, with one leg raised, immediately suggest movement and happiness.

Bagpipes provide the music for the dancing.

Country dancers, c. 1566

The Wedding Dance, by Dutch artist Pieter Bruegel the Elder, captures the high spirits and jollity of village festivities. He may be sending a message to the authorities, who at the time disapproved of energetic dancing.

The tutu is made of cotton and silk.

Rhythm and color, 1909–1911 and c. 1960

Gino Severini, an Italian painter, used color and pattern to give the idea of movement. *Dance of the Pan Pan at the "Monico"* is like looking through a kaleidoscope: the dancers splinter into bright geometric shapes that seem to shift, suggesting energy and rhythm.

Ballet student, c. 1881

French artist Edgar Degas depicts dance as beautiful but requiring great strength. His *Little Dancer Aged Fourteen* holds herself in an elegant pose. Degas' use of wax, clay, real hair, and clothing in a single sculpture broke new ground and makes the figure appear especially lifelike.

Dancing in the streets, 1935

Candombe is an exciting style of music and dance distinctive to Afro-Uruguayan culture. This dance originated from enslaved African people. Uruguayan artist Pedro Figari's colorful painting *Preparing the Candombe (Decoration)* presents a lively scene of men, women, and dogs getting ready for the dance. It creates a strong impression of shared identity and community spirit.

Jumping for joy, 1987

Using just five figures, six colors, and cartoon-style black lines, American artist Keith Haring captures the exhilaration of a group of dancers. *Untitled (Dance)* looks simple, but the effect is powerful: the picture bursts with movement and fun.

1820 ▶ 1830

Derby at Epsom

1822

The art of collecting

Charles Willson Peale was an American painter in the Neoclassical style who founded some of the first museums in the United States. In his self-portrait *The Artist in His Museum*, Peale proudly shows off the range of his collection, which included everything from dinosaur bones to stuffed birds.

The Artist in His Museum

1821

Motion in art

Théodore Géricault was a French Romantic painter known for dramatic scenes with lots of action. The race shown in the *Derby at Epsom* was a perfect subject for him, with the horses' bodies outstretched as they speed through the countryside. The approaching storm clouds add to the drama and excitement.

The instrument's bell is in the shape of a sea monster or dragon, called a chu-srin.

1800s

Tibetan trumpet

This copper trumpet, called a *rkangling*, comes from Tibet, and is decorated with coral and other stones. It was used to announce the arrival of ritual dancers. Originally, instruments like this were made from the thigh bone of a priest.

Tibetan rkangling

1820

1821

A simple country life

The title of the painting *The Hay Wain* by English artist John Constable refers to the wooden wain (wagon) used for transporting hay. As the wagon makes its way through the shallow stream, the focus here is on the beauty of the countryside. The painting represents a way of life that many people feared would be lost due to the arrival of towns and factories in the Industrial Revolution.

The Hay Wain

1827
Becoming a god
One of the great French Neoclassical artists was Jean-Auguste-Dominique Ingres. In *The Apotheosis of Homer*, he presents the ancient Greek poet Homer being crowned a god by Nike, the Greek goddess of victory. At his feet sit two objects that represent his most famous epic poems— a sword for the *Iliad*, and an oar for the *Odyssey*.

> **"It takes 25 years to learn to draw, one hour to learn to paint."**
> Jean-Auguste-Dominique Ingres, 1780–1867

The Apotheosis of Homer

1825

The artist carefully added the finer details of the leopard's spots, whiskers, and claws in black.

Leopard tureen

1800s
A leopard for a chief
European potteries often adapted their designs to suit buyers in Africa. This tureen (soup dish) was made for a buyer, possibly a chief, in the ancient kingdom of Kongo in central Africa. Leopards were a symbol of leadership in Africa because of their beauty and hunting skills, and this object may have been placed on the chief's grave to honor him.

Rattle in the form of a grouse

1800s
A ceremonial rattle
Skillfully shaped in the form of a grouse—a bird found across northern North America—this rattle was made by the Indigenous Makah people of the modern-day state of Washington. It was made from cedar wood, and designed based on dreams. Rattles like this were used in ceremonies.

Akan gold-weights
Gold dust was often used as money in the African countries of Ghana and Côte d'Ivoire. Small metal weights were made by the Akan people to measure the dust accurately. They came in many forms, such as this elephant.

The bird on the elephant's back refers to the Akan proverb about the safety of walking in an elephant's footsteps.

Elephant gold-weight with bird

The weight is made from brass.

1830

1830 ▶ 1840

📢 The Louvre opened in 1793, during the French Revolution, when thinkers in society demanded that royal art collections be made available to the public.

Gallery of the Louvre

1831–1833

A different display
Art galleries in the 1800s looked a little different from how they do today. In this painting of the Louvre Museum in Paris, France, American painter Samuel F. B. Morse shows us how the paintings were hung "salon style," meaning stacked in rows.

Eight Hundred Heroes of a Japanese Water Margin, All Told: Ogata Shuma Hiroyuki

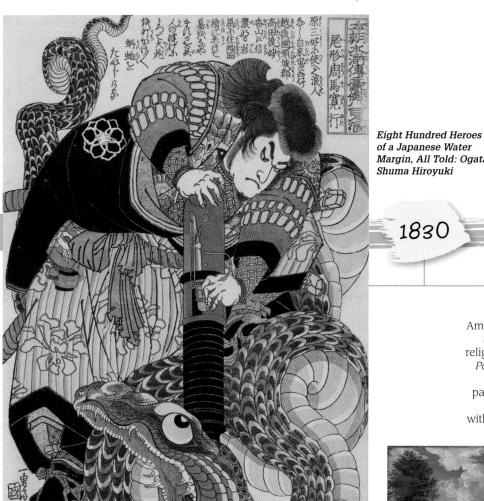

1830

c. 1830–1832

Peace on Earth
American painter Edward Hicks was also a member of the Quakers (a Christian religious group). He is well known for his *Peaceable Kingdom* paintings, which he painted in 62 different versions. The paintings represent an idea found in the Bible: the hope for harmony on Earth with all beings living together peacefully.

c. 1830

Protector of frogs
Japanese artist Utagawa Kuniyoshi is famed for his dramatic *ukiyo-e* art (see p.120) of warriors and heroes. His series *Eight Hundred Heroes of a Japanese Water Margin, All Told* includes this painting of the supernatural hero Jiraiya, who is killing a snake with a large weapon because it was scaring his friends, the frogs.

Peaceable Kingdom

Daguerreotype

In the 1830s, French artist Louis-Jacques-Mandé Daguerre developed the first widely available process of photography and called his photographs Daguerreotypes.

Camera used by Daguerre

1839

Sailing into history

A famous oil painting by English painter J. M. W. Turner, *The Fighting Temeraire* shows an old sailing ship on its final journey. It is being towed away by a steam-powered tug, smaller but faster vessels that were beginning to replace wooden ships. The sunset symbolizes not only the last of this ship's glory days, but the end of an era.

The Fighting Temeraire

1835 ───── **1840**

1835

Changing times

The invention of new technology powered the Industrial Revolution and changed peoples lives, as many moved from the country to work in factories in the cities. This watercolor by the English artist John Orlando Parry shows not only the smoggy, crowded city of London, but also the mass of information people were experiencing. New steam-powered presses could print posters and flyers faster and larger than ever before.

A London Street Scene

Carved figure with a protruding tongue, which was believed to part the seas as the canoe moved forward.

Māori canoe carvings

This 19th-century prow decorated the front of a Māori canoe (*waka*) from New Zealand. The elaborately carved figures are symbolic and were thought to give power to those on board.

127

Fishing Boats at Choshi in Shimosa

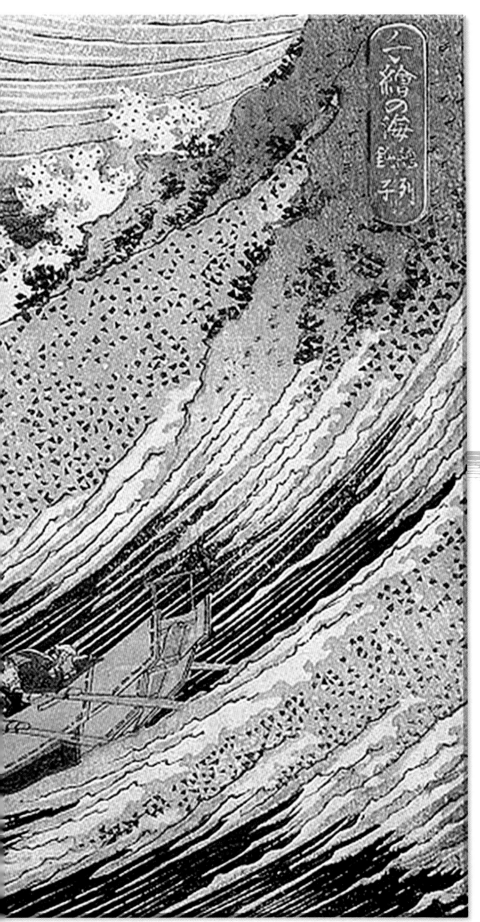

Hokusai's ocean

Fishing Boats at Choshi in Shimosa is a color woodblock print by the Japanese artist Katsushika Hokusai from his series *One Thousand Pictures of the Ocean*. With just a few simple black outlines and flat areas of color, Hokusai conveys a dramatic sweep of waves and the gurgling white foam of the ocean. It is made more intense by having no view of the horizon in the background. After Japan opened its ports to the West in 1854, prints like these circulated among European and American artists, and influenced the Modernist movement of the late 19th and early 20th centuries.

The largest of Hokusai's works is a collection of **4,000 sketches in 15 volumes,** called *Hokusai Manga*, published in 1814.

c. 1840–1900   REALISM

In the mid-19th century, the Realist movement came as a shock to the traditional art world. French artists such as Gustave Courbet and Jean-François Millet believed in painting the real world as it was around them, not just beautiful scenes, or stories from the Bible or ancient mythology, which were common subjects at the time. They went so far as to paint poor, dirty, and struggling people—those who were usually missing from traditional paintings.

Shocked audiences
In 1849, French painter Gustave Courbet depicted poor workers doing the backbreaking job of stone-breaking in his painting *The Stone Breakers*. People were shocked by his subject matter and could not understand why he wasted time painting such a dull, everyday scene.

Down in the dirt
Jean-François Millet also painted in the Realist style, as seen in *The Sower* from 1850. Audiences objected to the dull browns and grays in the painting and the poor farm worker as a subject, but Millet never stopped painting rural peasant life.

Art with purpose
With new design guidelines in England in the 1840s, objects started being decorated to match their purpose. Following these ideas, British artist Robert Redgrave decorated his *Well Spring* carafe with water reeds, because the container was used to hold water.

These leaves were painted with enamel, a glossy paint that hardens as it dries.

Well Spring **carafe**

1840

Plowing in the Nivernais

1849

Training her own way
This lifelike depiction of bulls plowing is by the French artist Rosa Bonheur, and reveals her real understanding of the structure of the great beasts' bodies. At this time, women were not allowed the same art training as men, so to learn animal anatomy, Bonheur studied in the butcher's shop.

Painting the landscape

In *Green Mountains and Red Trees, after Lu Zhi*, Chinese painter Gu Kui paints a landscape of forests and steep mountains shrouded in fog in the style of 16th-century artist Lu Zhi. In the foreground are some houses at the base of a waterfall, obscured by a thicket of trees. This is an example of Chinese album leaf art—small paintings that could fit inside an album or a book.

Green Mountains and Red Trees, after Lu Zhi

Akan badge

This intricately decorated gold pendant is an *akrafokonmu* ("soulwasher's badge") from the Asante Kingdom in modern-day Ghana. It was worn by special attendants to the king to protect his spiritual well-being and the kingdom.

The concentric patterns represent the rays of the sun, which held great significance to the king.

Soulwasher's Badge

1850

1849–1850

Simpler times

English painter Dante Gabriel Rossetti was one of the artists who established the Pre-Raphaelite Brotherhood in 1848. This group of artists disliked the technology brought about by the Industrial Revolution. Rossetti painted *Ecce Ancilla Domini!*, a Christian scene of the Annunciation (see pp.66–67), instead of painting a contemporary scene with factories and railroad cars.

Season's greetings

The world's first Christmas card was introduced in 1843 after British art specialist Sir Henry Cole came up with the idea of sending illustrated greeting cards at Christmas time. It shows a family raising a toast and scenes of charity.

Ecce Ancilla Domini! (The Annunciation)

1850 ▸ 1860

The marble has been skillfully carved to look like creases in the clothing.

Painted and
lacquered
book cover

1852

Fighting for her country

The 15th-century warrior Joan of Arc claimed that angels and saints had told her to lead France in the Hundred Years' War against England. In this marble statue, French sculptor François Rude shows the young girl listening intently for heavenly inspiration, while her battle armor lies close at hand.

Joan of Arc

c. 1850s

Multicultural art

This decorative book cover from Persia combines styles and techniques from several cultures. A Persian artist has painted Christian scenes in a typically European style. A liquid called resin was then applied to the cover, which hardened into a glossy, protective surface. This technique, called lacquering, originally came from China.

1850

1855

The original Delaware painting was destroyed during World War II, but luckily Emanuel Leutze painted several versions.

A cold wind whips back the American flag.

Washington Crossing the Delaware

1851

A revolutionary moment

German-American artist Emanuel Leutze created this imposing 21-ft- (6.5-m-) long painting to celebrate an important turning point in the American Revolution. It shows General George Washington leading American troops across the icy Delaware River to launch a surprise attack on enemy forces.

1856

Setting a standard

During the 1840s, art specialist Sir Henry Cole campaigned to improve the quality of British-made goods. In response, British designer Owen Jones put together a book of patterns and decorations from across the world, called *The Grammar of Ornament*, for use by designers when creating their work.

A page from *The Grammar of Ornament*

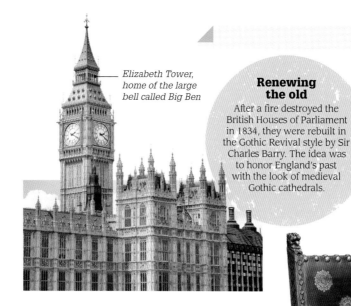

Elizabeth Tower, home of the large bell called Big Ben

Renewing the old

After a fire destroyed the British Houses of Parliament in 1834, they were rebuilt in the Gothic Revival style by Sir Charles Barry. The idea was to honor England's past with the look of medieval Gothic cathedrals.

1859

Gothic revival

In the rapidly modernizing world of the 19th century, an architectural movement grew that looked to Gothic style for inspiration (see p.49). English architect and designer, A. W. N. Pugin, a leading figure of the Gothic Revival movement, also incorporated the style in furniture. The legs of this chair feature pointed arches.

1860

Quilting art

This colorful quilt was made by or for Susan Holbert, who lived in rural New York State in the mid-1850s. At this time, women were largely excluded from art schools, but quilt-making was a creative art they could pursue.

1797–1858   UTAGAWA HIROSHIGE

Born Andō Tokutarō, Japanese artist Utagawa Hiroshige acquired his name from his teacher, Utagawa Toyohiro. Hiroshige was a great master of woodblock prints in the *ukiyo-e* style (see p.103), and was admired for his ability to capture the beauty of nature in calm landscapes and scenes showing changing seasons. His work was also popular in Europe and the US, where it inspired many Impressionist artists.

Spring blossoms

Made in 1857, Hiroshige's woodblock print *Plum Garden in Kamata* is a part of his series *One Hundred Famous Views of Edo*, which featured scenes from popular locations around Tokyo. This colourful scene shows people enjoying an early spring evening among blossoming plum trees.

Contrasting lives

The fine clothing of the two women contrasts with the tatty rags of the poor plant seller at the front, who—lacking education—is doing the only work open to him. The figure in a purple bonnet is distributing religious pamphlets, a kind of work taken on by many middle-class women.

Taking a break

This hot worker quenches his thirst with a large beer. At this time, the working classes did not always have access to clean drinking water, making beer an often safer choice. These laborers are the painting's heroes, and the artist presents them as noble and strong.

Street children

The black ribbons tied to the baby's sleeves suggest that someone close to these children has recently died—probably their mother. Now their big sister has to take charge of the family. Her tattered dress, though still quite fancy, is far too big for her, and was probably given to her by a charity.

Changing times
Work, 1852–1865, Ford Madox Brown

Ford Madox Brown was a British painter associated with the Pre-Raphaelites (see p.131), sharing the movement's use of vivid colors and interest in social themes. Though the central focus of this masterpiece is a group of laborers busily digging up a London street, almost everyone in the painting is doing work of some kind—and through it Brown delivers a moral message about the importance of labor. The scene also brings together rich and poor to contrast their very different lives.

The "Holy Family"
Despite their poverty, this homeless couple's main concern is the care of their baby. The woman's bonnet looks like a halo, suggesting a link to depictions of Mary and the infant Jesus in Christian art.

Brainworkers
Brown included portraits of two real-life thinkers he admired: Thomas Carlyle and F. D. Maurice. They wrote about the vital importance of work and education. Brown called them "brainworkers."

1860 ▶ 1870

c. 1863

Magic in marble

This bust of a nun was made as a showpiece, intended to impress people with the sculptor's skill. The Italian artist, possibly Giuseppe Croff, has created from marble the magical effect of a thin, semitransparent veil over the woman's face.

The marble has been expertly transformed into delicate folds of fabric.

1800s

Whalebone carving

This long, flat object is a scrimshaw—a carving made on whalebone, typically done by sailors who hunted whales. Whaling crews spent long months at sea, so carving was a way for them to pass the time. This particular example is a busk—something that was inserted into a woman's corset in order to stiffen it—so it may have been intended as a gift to a loved one back home.

 Traditionally, artists made busts in clay or plaster before a master craftsperson turned their work into stone.

The Veiled Nun

1860

Scrimshaw whale busk

The tall ship is shown sailing away.

1864–1865

New style

French artist Édouard Manet frequently broke away from traditional styles to find new and different ways to paint. *Peonies* shows his use of loose, unfinished-looking brushstrokes and blobs of paint that were considered quite shocking in his time.

❝There are no lines in nature, only areas of color, one against another.❞

Édouard Manet, 1832–1883

Peonies

Among the Sierra Nevada, California

America the beautiful

German-American artist Albert Bierstadt's panoramic painting *Among the Sierra Nevada, California* idealizes the American countryside as a beautiful paradise. Radiant sunlight and brightly lit clouds create a dramatic interplay of light and shadow on an unspoiled landscape. Bierstadt's paintings went on tour in Europe, where they enticed people to travel to America to start a new life.

1865   1870 ▶▶

Tenniel's illustration for *Alice's Adventures in Wonderland*

1865

Book illustration

During the 19th century, children's books had mostly black-and-white illustrations. English artist John Tenniel created the illustrations for English author Lewis Carroll's novel *Alice's Adventures in Wonderland*. He depicted many fantastical scenes, such as this one of an oversize Alice watching a rabbit run away.

PAINTING OUTDOORS

In the 1870s, artists such as Claude Monet, Édouard Manet, and Gustave Courbet began to paint entire artworks outside instead of in the studio. This was an unusual practice, but painting *en plein air* (in the open air) allowed artists to capture the changing effects of light and the weather more clearly. The technique became fundamental to Impressionism (see p.141).

Courbet at work

This photograph shows French artist Gustave Courbet painting in a garden. The invention of metal tubes for oil paints made painting outside much easier.

Sisley's snowy scene

By painting *Early Snow at Louveciennes* (1870–1871) outside, French artist Alfred Sisley could capture the fleeting quality of the changing seasons.

Colors of ice

A painting of ice may be expected to be mostly white, but Church has added more colors here. He had studied nature closely, and realized that water and ice reflected the colors around them.

Distant icebergs

Icebergs and ice caps are visible as far as the eye can see. They signal that the waters may look calm and still, but these are treacherous seas.

Beware!

The broken mast of a wrecked ship juts out from the bottom of this lifeless scene. It shows the viewer how massive those icebergs really are, and warns them of what can happen here.

A chilling scene

The Icebergs, 1861, Frederic Edwin Church

American artist Frederic Edwin Church was a Romantic painter, and was a part of the Hudson River School, a group of artists who celebrated the power of nature through dramatic landscapes. Church was known for the detail in his paintings. For *The Icebergs*, he traveled to northern Canada to study the freezing terrain up close, braving dangerous icy waters in a tiny rowing boat to create this foreboding yet beautiful picture.

Stormy skies

Many Romantic painters used stormy skies in the backgrounds of their works. Church also takes the opportunity to include danger and excitement with these rolling thunderclouds.

Solitary rock

A craggy rock peeks out from underneath the ice, a reminder that this place is unpredictable and dangerous. Any boat passing underneath risked being crushed if the rock fell.

The chilly water

There are no huge waves crashing into the shoreline here. Instead, tiny ripples in the murky water bring a cold stillness to this picture, which is even more ominous.

Mysterious grotto

Although his paintings look real, Church included some details from his imagination. This grotto (cave) might not have been there in real life, but Church knew the intense turquoise color and underwater glow would catch the eye.

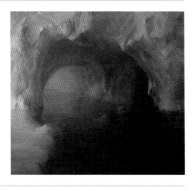

1870 ▶ 1880

An up-turned snout reveals sharp teeth and a long, wiggly tongue.

Late 1800s
Golden ring
This intricate gold ring was designed for Thai royalty. Although it is shaped like an intimidating serpent with bulging eyes, it represents a divine creature from South Asia called a *naga*. These supernatural beings were believed to guard pearls and corals in the underworld.

The ring is made of 22-carat gold.

Naga ring

The Dance Class

1874
Ballet practice
French artist Edgar Degas applied Impressionist techniques to his many paintings of ballet dancers—one of his favorite subjects. The small, thin brushstrokes were the perfect choice for the gauzy tutus and ribbons worn by the ballerinas as they practiced.

1870

1871
Subtle shades
Many people think this painting is about a son's love for his mother. In fact, though he and his mother were very close, American artist James McNeill Whistler said this painting of her was a study of the subtle differences between the shades of black, gray, and white.

Arrangement in Gray and Black, No 1: The Artist's Mother

The flowers and birds are painted in watercolor.

Mirror case of the Qajar Period

1874
Lacquered cover
Decorated mirror cases were popular during the Qajar Dynasty in Persia (modern-day Iran). The lacquer coating on top of the watercolor and gold image gives the case its glossy sheen and protects it from wear and tear.

c. 1860–1880   IMPRESSIONISM

In the 1860s and 1870s, some French artists began to paint in a style considered radical by many because of the unfinished look of their loose, sketchy brushstrokes. This style came to be called Impressionism and it soon spread to other countries. Major art schools and galleries rejected this style, so the Impressionists set up their own independent exhibitions of their work.

Landscapes and light
Impressionists painted snapshots or "impressions" of landscapes and everyday life, often outdoors, instead of depicting historical or religious topics. In *The Red Roofs* (1877), French artist Camille Pissaro translated the changing light and weather into vibrant colors on the canvas.

1875   1880

1877

Under a spell
British artist Edward Burne-Jones was a part of the Pre-Raphaelite Brotherhood who looked to the past for inspiration (see also p.131). In this work, he painted the wizard Merlin from the legend of King Arthur, falling under a sleeping spell cast by the Lady of the Lake, Nimue.

Curved leaves and swirling stems were colored by hand.

Pimpernel **wallpaper by Morris & Co**

1876

Bringing nature indoors
British artist William Morris led the Arts and Crafts movement, a group that championed handmade rather than factory-made goods. They focused on the beauty of nature in their works, such as in this wallpaper.

Detailed folds of cloth flow down the body like water.

The Beguiling of Merlin

An afternoon party

Dance at Le Moulin de la Galette, 1876, Pierre-Auguste Renoir

Impressionists painted scenes of everyday life using bright colors and quick, imprecise brushstrokes. One impressive example is *Dance at Le Moulin de la Galette* by French artist Pierre-Auguste Renoir. The painting brings to life a beautiful Sunday afternoon at an outdoor dance club in Paris, France. This subject was a perfect choice for an Impressionist, because the artist could explore the way sunlight moved across the dance floor, people's faces, and their clothes. Renoir's work beautifully captures the way bright light shining on objects lightens or changes their colors.

Who's that girl?
Impressionists painted the world around them, which means their works often included people they knew in real life. The girl in the blue-and-pink striped dress is Estelle, the sister of French actress Jeanne Samary, who posed for Renoir's paintings many times.

A private conversation
Near the center of this painting, a young man leans over to speak to a young woman. Is he asking for a dance? Renoir has captured a mysterious, fleeting moment in a busy scene.

Dancers in the distance

Impressionist artists did not spend much time on tiny details—they had to work quickly to capture the changing light and mood of a scene. A closer look at this painting reveals that most of the dancers in the background are nothing more than a few quick swipes of the paintbrush. But when the painting is viewed as a whole, the vague, sketchy brushstrokes make sense.

Hat fashion

Straw hats were a popular fashion for the ordinary, working-class people in this painting who are enjoying a day off. In a fancier dance club or at a ball, upper-class men would wear black top hats.

Patches of sun

Renoir makes this painting seem to sparkle, with patches of sunlight peeking through the tree branches overhead. It is not hard to imagine sunny patches, such as those on this man's dark jacket, shifting and shimmering with every gentle breeze.

> **"I have placed there a little door opening on to the mysterious. I have made stories."**
>
> Odilon Redon, 1840–1916

The Winged Man

1880

Mysterious symbols

French artist Odilon Redon was part of the Symbolist movement, which used imaginative imagery that often did not make sense to anyone but themselves. Redon's work has a rather spooky, dreamlike quality, such as in this depiction of a winged man.

1881

Official stamp

This ivory seal from China was used to stamp papers, art, or anything requiring a label or a signature. It has different texts and images on each of its six sides. These delicate engravings are a work of art in themselves.

This face shows a man in a landscape of bamboo.

Six-sided seal

1880

1880

Deep in thought

French artist Auguste Rodin is the first truly Modernist sculptor. Modernism was a movement that sought to reflect the new industrialized society, often using different kinds of subjects, materials, and techniques to create art. Rodin's most famous work, *The Thinker*, was a radical change from the usual heroic sculptures of kings and generals. Rugged and expressive, it is cast in bronze.

The Thinker

1882

Reviving old traditions

Bird and Willow in Snow by Japanese artist Shibata Zeshin is a Nihonga painting from Japan's Meiji Period. While younger artists learned Western techniques, Nihonga painters returned to traditional elements of Japanese art, such as asymmetry and simplicity.

Bird and Willow in Snow

1841–1895   BERTHE MORISOT

French painter Berthe Morisot was a leading member of the Impressionist movement at a time when there were still very few female artists. Her family allowed her to study formally, and her most well-known works are intimate, brightly colored scenes of women and children at home—subjects that were rarely chosen by male artists.

Sunflowers

Posing at the piano

Lucie Léon at the Piano (1892) shows Morisot's use of loose slashes of paint. The Impressionist style was ideal for capturing the soft textures of the girl's hair, her dress, and the delicate flowers on top of the piano.

1888
Bold textures
Dutch artist Vincent Van Gogh painted several versions of *Sunflowers*. This series not only demonstrates his love for vivid colors, but also his use of the technique known as *impasto,* where bumpy, thick layers of paint are applied for a textured effect.

1885   1890

When viewed from a distance, yellow and blue dots next to each other combine to produce a third color—green.

A Sunday Afternoon on the Island of La Grande Jatte

1884–1886
Painting with dots
French artist Georges Seurat painted using millions of tiny dots or points of color to create a sort of optical illusion. This new style, which he invented, came to be known as Pointillism. His paintings reflect his understanding of how colors are seen by the eye—different-colored dots blend together when seen from afar.

Still life

A painting that shows arrangements of objects such as vases, food, and flowers, usually on a table, is known as a still life. This style of painting can be traced right back to ancient Egypt, but still life only really took off as an art form in the 16th century. A still life gives artists lots of freedom—they can choose which objects to depict, and experiment with different techniques. It is also a great opportunity to show off their skills.

Burial offerings, c. 1400–1342 BCE
This painting from a 3,500-year-old tomb in Egypt shows crops, fish, and bowls of fruit. The ancient Egyptians believed that when they died they would travel to the afterlife. They painted their tombs with everything they would need for the next world.

New perspectives, 1893
In *The Basket of Apples*, by French artist Paul Cézanne, some of the fruit looks in danger of tumbling off the table. This is because Cézanne experimented with painting objects as if seeing them from different angles at the same time, to show them in three dimensions. It also explains why the table edges do not line up.

Reflections of light on the pewter pitcher are skillfully captured.

The olives are served in an expensive Chinese porcelain bowl.

Extravagant feast, 1627
Still Life with a Peacock Pie by Dutch painter Pieter Claesz shows a table laid with luxurious imported foods. Each item highlights the artist's skill at depicting different textures, from bumpy lemon peel to glinting metal.

The paint is applied quickly and freely.

Master of disguise, 1915

The Cubist artist Juan Gris, from Spain, played games with his paintings. *Still Life with Checked Tablecloth* shows a table full of cups, bottles—even a guitar. Or does it? The items are arranged in such a way that they also make up a bull's head.

Sad flowers, 1918

One of the leading members of the German Expressionist movement, Ernst Ludwig Kirchner used strong colors and thick brushstrokes in a way that expressed emotion. The dark background of *Pink Roses* emphasizes the flowers, but also gives the painting a rather sad feel— perhaps suggesting their beauty is short-lived.

Lavish table, 1920

The French artist Raoul Dufy said he painted scenes "the way I see things with my eyes and in my heart." This energetic still life shows a table laden with food and drink. The two-dimensional bowls and glass objects show Dufy's interest in Cubism, while the rich colors—especially his favorite, blue—show Fauvist influence (see pp.152–153).

Sweet treats, 1962

American painter Wayne Thiebaud is known for his colorful artwork depicting the delicious foods he grew up with. *Confections* shows a row of tempting ice-cream sundaes in different-shaped glasses. Thiebaud used a knife to spread the paint thickly, helping to suggest the texture of cream.

1890 ▶ 1900

Fear that echoes

Norwegian artist Edvard Munch's famous painting *The Scream* is an example of Expressionism—a style of painting that aimed to provoke emotion in the viewer. In it a skeletal figure cradles his face with his hands as he lets out a blood-curdling cry. The viewer is left to imagine what might be so terrifying as the wavy lines of his scream echo throughout the landscape.

> **"No longer shall I paint interiors ... I will paint living people who breathe and feel and suffer and love."**
>
> Edvard Munch, 1863–1944

The Scream

▶▶ 1890 ─────────────────────●────────────── 1895

1890

Rural life

French painter Paul Gauguin was fascinated with people who lived a simple farm life, away from the hustle and bustle of the city. He depicts this rural scene in Brittany, France, using bands of color and simplified forms. Some parts almost look like pieces of stained glass.

Haystacks in Brittany

Mont Sainte-Victoire

1892–1895

Patchwork of colors

The art movement that followed Impressionism was called Post-Impressionism, and artists explored different styles. French artist Paul Cézanne had painted this mountain many times and sought to simplify what he saw. In this version, he used little blocks of colors, like a patchwork quilt, to depict the mountain—featuring a mix of lifelike gray and brown, as well as shades of pink, orange, and green.

c. 1890–1910   ART NOUVEAU

The 1890s saw the rise of the Art Nouveau ("New Art") movement, in which artists used flowing, asymmetrical shapes and designs inspired by nature and the simple lines of Japanese woodblock prints (see p.103). Artists also began to use the Art Nouveau style for posters, advertisements, and magazine illustrations, making many wonder if these objects should be considered serious artistic creations.

Eye-catching poster
Czech artist Alphonse Mucha was known for his theater posters, such as this one from 1908 advertising the work of the silent film and stage actress Leslie Carter. Mucha celebrates nature with the delicate patterns and sweeping curves of the Art Nouveau style.

The folds in the fabric mimic the look of flower petals.

Flowing lines
The influence of Japan is clear in the delicate lines of *The Peacock Skirt* (1894) by British artist Aubrey Beardsley. This drawing in typically fluid Art Nouveau style is one of 16 made by Beardsley to illustrate the first English edition of *Salome*, a play by Irish writer Oscar Wilde.

A long peacock feather winds its way down the page.

1900

The pale moonlight adds to the unreal quality of the scene.

The Sleeping Gypsy

1897

Quiet danger
Symbolist painters like French artist Henri Rousseau made art full of mystery and fantasy. In *The Sleeping Gypsy*, there is a sense of danger as a lion sniffs around a sleeping musician. The dreamlike quality of this still landscape makes the viewer wonder if the lion is real or a figment of the musician's imagination.

1800s

Safety of home
The Sentani people of Papua, Indonesia, live in villages built over the waters of Lake Sentani, using wooden posts to support their homes. In the 19th century, the tops of the posts supporting the chief's house would have carvings like this one of a mother and child. This subject brings to mind feelings of home, family, and security.

The child is held safely by the mother.

Carved wooden house post of a mother and child

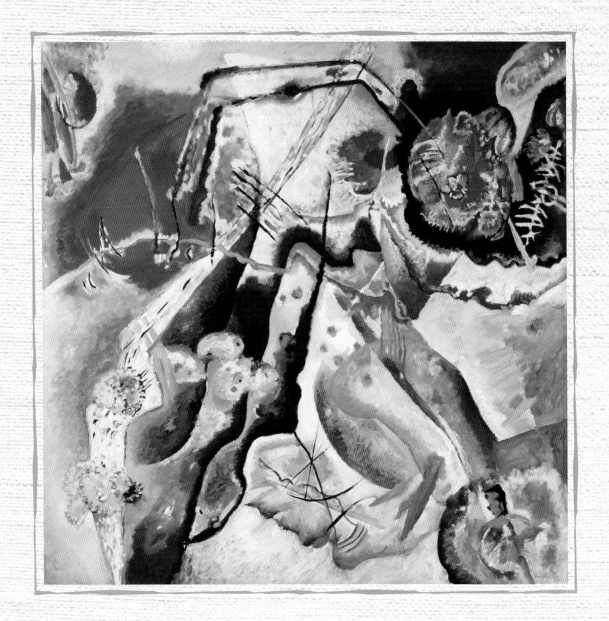

1900–present

At the start of the 20th century, many artists moved away from the kinds of art that had been made before, in ways that sometimes shocked viewers. They began to create bolder works, often using new media such as photography, collage, and film. Some of these questioned what it actually means for something to be "art," while later on, others pushed the boundaries still further by borrowing from advertising, or creating installations—art that people could participate in. Over the course of this period, artists who had largely been overlooked—such as women, and Black and Indigenous people—gained the recognition they have long deserved.

1900 ▶ 1910

Yup'ik
artifact

1906
Bold new style
A new art style called Fauvism (meaning "wild beasts" in French) saw artists use bright colors in small dabs and strokes to create simple, lively shapes. In his portrait of fellow Fauvist André Derain, French painter Maurice de Vlaminck uses bold brushstrokes in unrealistic colors to highlight his friend's features.

André Derain

c. 1900
Alaskan celebration
During long Arctic winters, the Yup'ik people of Alaska gathered in ceremonial houses to feast and dance. Objects crafted with painted driftwood and feathers were hung from the ceiling to honor the animals that had been hunted for the feast. This one depicts a figure in a kayak made to resemble a walrus.

▶▶ **1900** — **1905**

1902
Lights, camera, action!
The invention of the moving picture allowed people to explore artistic ideas in a new way. French filmmaker Georges Méliès made a short film called *A Trip to the Moon* 67 years before the first moon landing, and used weird and wonderful set designs for this space adventure. The film was painstakingly colored by hand.

Gold leaf
Gold, a precious metal, can be hammered down into fine sheets, called gold leaf. Artists use these sheets to decorate their paintings or objects. This process is called gilding.

A still from *A Trip to the Moon*

> ❝Art is a line around your thoughts.❞
>
> Gustav Klimt, 1862–1918

Bread and Fruit Bowl on a Table

1881–1962 NATALIA GONCHAROVA

Russian artist Natalia Goncharova's early paintings are inspired by the people of her homeland, and feature landscape scenes depicting the rural life of peasants. Russian folk art as well as traditional children's toys were a source of inspiration for her work, and helped express a unique Russian identity. Goncharova was also influenced by Cubism, a style she used in her paintings between 1910 and 1914.

Vibrant scenes
Peasant women can be seen planting flowers in Goncharova's bold and patterned *Gardening* (1908), an example of early Russian Modernism.

1908

Leading a movement

Spanish artist Pablo Picasso, together with the French painter Georges Braque, created a new style of art called Cubism. They used angular geometric shapes rather than natural lines to show people or objects, as in Picasso's *Bread and Fruit Bowl on a Table*. Cubism shocked the world, but inspired many artists to experiment with different ways of representing reality.

1907

1910 ▸▸

Fallen Leaves

1909

A changing landscape

Japanese artist Hishida Shunso created a new style of art by adding pale gradients of color to simple landscapes. The effect made his works appear to glow, a quality that had not been seen before in Japanese art. *Fallen Leaves*, made on a folding screen, received the Japan Art Academy's highest award in 1911.

1907

Painted in gold

Gold and silver leaf decorate *Portrait of Adele Bloch-Bauer*. Its creator, Austrian artist Gustav Klimt, was known for his gilded, ornamental paintings. In this work, he has depicted this wealthy society hostess and art patron in a geometric dress inspired by ancient mosaics and Egyptian artifacts.

Portrait of Adele Bloch-Bauer

153

1910 ▶ 1920

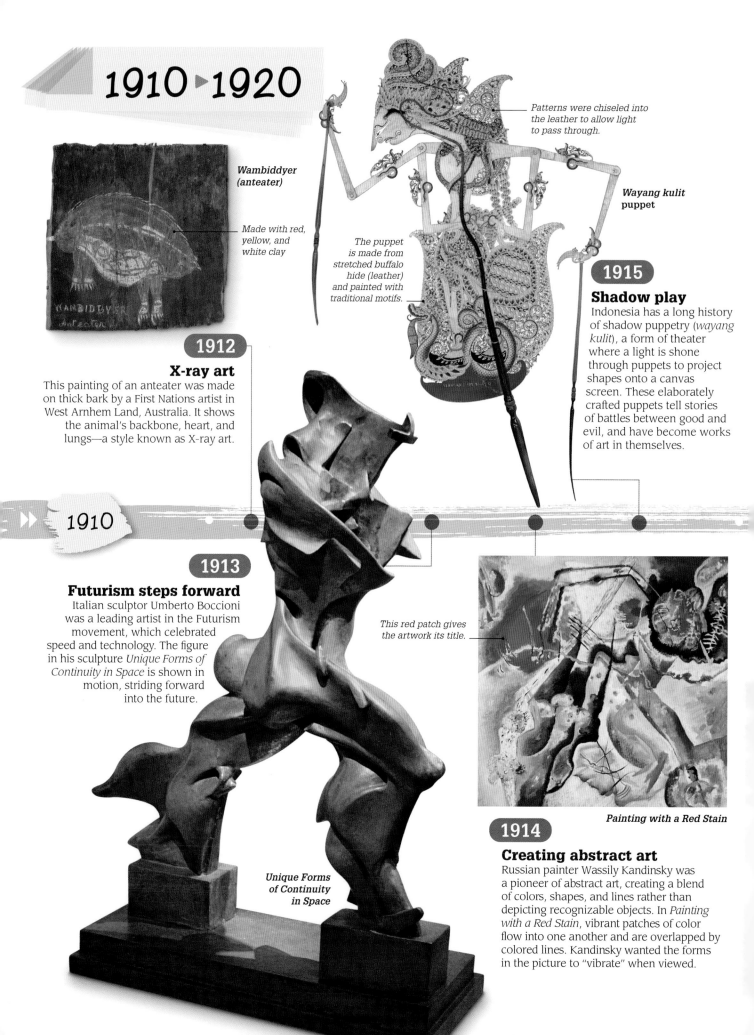

Wambiddyer (anteater)

Made with red, yellow, and white clay

Patterns were chiseled into the leather to allow light to pass through.

Wayang kulit puppet

The puppet is made from stretched buffalo hide (leather) and painted with traditional motifs.

1915
Shadow play
Indonesia has a long history of shadow puppetry (*wayang kulit*), a form of theater where a light is shone through puppets to project shapes onto a canvas screen. These elaborately crafted puppets tell stories of battles between good and evil, and have become works of art in themselves.

1912
X-ray art
This painting of an anteater was made on thick bark by a First Nations artist in West Arnhem Land, Australia. It shows the animal's backbone, heart, and lungs—a style known as X-ray art.

1910

1913
Futurism steps forward
Italian sculptor Umberto Boccioni was a leading artist in the Futurism movement, which celebrated speed and technology. The figure in his sculpture *Unique Forms of Continuity in Space* is shown in motion, striding forward into the future.

Unique Forms of Continuity in Space

This red patch gives the artwork its title.

Painting with a Red Stain

1914
Creating abstract art
Russian painter Wassily Kandinsky was a pioneer of abstract art, creating a blend of colors, shapes, and lines rather than depicting recognizable objects. In *Painting with a Red Stain*, vibrant patches of color flow into one another and are overlapped by colored lines. Kandinsky wanted the forms in the picture to "vibrate" when viewed.

"I have always tried to exploit the photograph. I use it like color, or as the poet uses the word."

Hannah Höch, 1889–1978

1919

Photomontage
German artist Hannah Höch combined images and headlines cut from newspapers and magazines to make her artworks, in a style known as photomontage. The fragmented images in this example reflect how turbulent and broken society was after World War I.

Cut with the Kitchen Knife Dada through the Last Weimar Beer-Belly Cultural Epoch of Germany

1920

1918

The world at war
With the outbreak of World War I in 1914, many artists began to document the reality of war. *Over the Top* by British artist John Nash is based on his own experience, and depicts soldiers clambering out of snowy trenches during a winter attack.

Over the Top

c. 1900s   ASSEMBLAGE

The technique of making art from everyday objects or scrap materials is known as assemblage. Some artists joined objects together to form a sort of three-dimensional collage (as in Naum Gabo's *Head of a Woman* below). Early works transformed the art world of the time because they challenged people's ideas of what art was.

Readymade
Fountain was one of French artist Marcel Duchamp's "readymades"—everyday objects turned into art. The white urinal, signed "R Mutt" to disguise the artist's identity, was rejected in 1917 by the Society of Independent Artists, who refused to consider it a work of art.

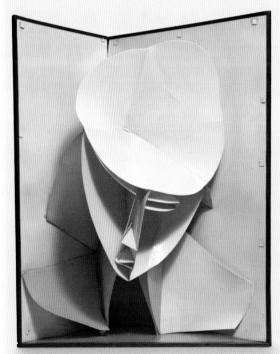

Constructing art
Head of a Woman (1917–1920) by Russian artist Naum Gabo might at first glance look like it was made from the folded pages of a book, but it is, in fact, a sculpture made from plastic and metal.

Blending reality and fantasy

I and the Village, 1911, Marc Chagall

Russian-born artist Marc Chagall painted *I and the Village* while he was living in Paris, France. Thinking back to the home he left behind, Chagall combines childhood memories from his village in Russia, Jewish folk tales, and his thoughts on nature to create this dreamlike scene. The artist was inspired by both Cubism and Fauvism (see pp.152–153), which can be seen in his use of angular shapes and an unusual color palette.

Milking a goat
Remembering the everyday life of his childhood, Chagall paints a woman milking a goat. The scene symbolizes the way peasants lived in harmony with animals, and reminds the viewer that nature is the source of life.

Tree of Life
A flowering branch bursting with seeds represents the Tree of Life, a symbol of life and rebirth. Placed between the artist and the goat, it suggests the need for a balanced relationship between humans, animals, and plants.

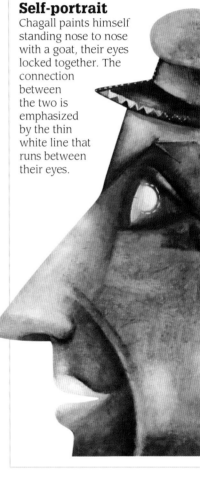

Self-portrait
Chagall paints himself standing nose to nose with a goat, their eyes locked together. The connection between the two is emphasized by the thin white line that runs between their eyes.

Farmer and musician
The laws of gravity are suspended as a farmer walking uphill comes across an upside-down woman playing an invisible violin. Chagall often included floating figures in his paintings, giving them an air of magic.

A street scene
This street with houses and an Orthodox church is inspired by Chagall's hometown of Vitebsk (in modern-day Belarus). The artist adds a dreamlike effect to the street by including a giant face and brightly colored upside-down buildings.

Abstract shapes create a human face.

1920

Dadaism

Angered by the loss of life during World War I, a group of artists started an "anti-art" movement called Dada. Artists would create playful works that mixed together different materials, as seen in this painted, wooden *Dada Head* by Swiss artist Sophie Taeuber-Arp.

Dada Head

Harlequin's Carnival

1924

Paintings run wild

Spanish artist Joan Miró experimented with "automatic painting," allowing his subconscious mind to take over while creating. This technique produced some weird and wonderful outcomes, such as *Harlequin's Carnival*, which shows wiggly animals and people singing and dancing.

1920 ▶▶

1922

Paul Klee at the Bauhaus

Swiss-German artist Paul Klee taught for 10 years at the Bauhaus art school in Germany—one of the first schools to teach modern design. During this time, he experimented with mixing colors. In his watercolor *Three Houses*, several pairs of colors, including violet and green, are blended together to create a blue-gray shade.

Three Houses

A Morning in May and Me before Breakfast

1923

Mavo movement

The artists of the Mavo movement, led by Japanese artist Murayama Tomoyoshi, rebelled against traditional art styles and took inspiration from modern industrial shapes. An example is this painting by Masamu Yanase, where the artist has created a spiral cityscape. Lines and zig-zags have been scratched into the paint to add texture.

1928

Painter of her country

Modernist artist Tarsila do Amaral's life ambition was to paint her home country of Brazil. Her bold and vibrant artwork, such as *Abaporu*, shows landscapes filled with cacti and the hot sun beating down. This work also shows the influence of Surrealism, which she encountered on a trip to Europe.

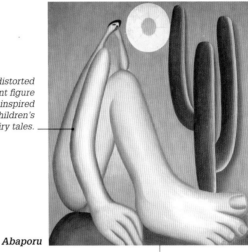

This distorted giant figure is inspired by children's fairy tales.

Abaporu

Cast turned into a canvas with brightly colored drawings of branches and flowers

Painted body cast

1925

Art on bandage

At the age of 18, Mexican artist Frida Kahlo was involved in a terrible bus accident, which left her bedridden with a back injury. During her recovery, she discovered painting and began expressing her pain through art. She even decorated her plaster body casts, transforming them into beautiful artworks.

1925 ●　　　　●　　●　　　　●　　　●　1930 ▶▶

1920s–1930s ART DECO

Named after the International Exhibition of Modern Decorative and Industrial Arts held in Paris, France, in 1925, Art Deco symbolized elegance, luxury, and all things modern. This art style combined geometric patterns and sleek, streamlined shapes. Art Deco influenced the design of many things, from fashion and architecture to cars and ocean liners.

Painting

Typical of Art Deco, this glamorous self-portrait was originally created for the cover of a 1929 magazine. The Polish artist Tamara de Lempicka portrayed herself as a successful modern-day woman with bright red lips and long leather driving gloves, speeding past in a green sports car.

The painting uses sophisticated but bold colors.

Self-portrait in a Green Bugatti

Architecture

Built in 1930, the Chrysler Building in New York City was briefly the tallest building in the world. Its sunburst design and the use of materials such as stainless steel make it a classic example of Art Deco architecture.

Jewelery

Art Deco jewelery used diamonds and gemstones in strong contrasting colors. Small clusters of stones made up designs inspired by images such as Egyptian artifacts, animals, and plants.

Brooch with diamonds, rubies, and emeralds

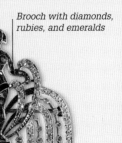

Human sculptures

Throughout the history of art, sculptures of people have always had a special fascination—as humans ourselves, we instantly try to imagine the character and their life. Some human sculptures depict specific figures from history or legend; others make us question what it is to be human by the shape and style of their design. Often, artists simplify or exaggerate parts of the body to create a specific effect.

Ancient scribe, c. 2500 BCE

This painted sculpture from ancient Egypt depicts a scribe (someone who wrote official documents). He looks alert, sitting with his right hand hovering as if ready to write. The statue may have been placed in the tomb of a pharaoh to serve him in the afterlife.

Figure of legend, Date unknown

Stone *nomoli* figurines such as this one have been found in Sierra Leone and Guinea. Their original purpose remains a mystery, but it is thought they may have represented ancient kings or characters from legends.

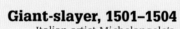
Slingshot

Giant-slayer, 1501–1504

Italian artist Michelangelo's famous *David* was inspired by a story from the Bible. It shows the hero preparing to fight the giant Goliath, armed with only a slingshot. Michelangelo studied how the muscles of the body worked, and the imposing figure—14 ft (4.3 m) high—is very detailed and realistic.

Beaming smile, c. 600–800 CE

Sculptors from the Remojadas culture (in modern-day Mexico) made many smiling figures like this one—but no one knows why. With his wide smile and sticking-out tongue, he may symbolize the trancelike state achieved during religious rituals.

The serene expression creates an impression of balance and beauty.

Golden curves, 1913

Mlle Pogany, version 1, by Romanian sculptor Constantin Brâncuși, is not a realistic portrait. Instead, the model's face, eyes, nose, and hair are all shown using smooth, stylized curves. The simplified shapes and exaggerated eyes suggest influence by African and Buddhist sculptural forms.

Home comfort 1949–1951

Family Group, by British artist Henry Moore, shows a mother and father sitting on a bench, holding a child between them. The shape of the sculpture, with the child enveloped by the parents' bodies, suggests family protection and togetherness.

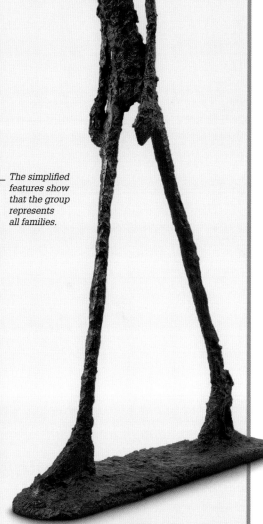

The bronze sculpture stands almost 6 ft (2 m) tall.

The simplified features show that the group represents all families.

Thin man, 1960

Swiss artist Alberto Giacometti is known for his long, thin figures. *Walking Man I* strides forward purposefully, but Giacometti has elongated his arms and legs until they look ready to snap. It suggests human beings are both strong and fragile.

1930 ▶ 1940

Jimson Weed/White Flower No. 1

1932
Painting nature
US artist Georgia O'Keeffe is known for celebrating the simple beauty of nature in her paintings of flowers. In this large painting, O'Keeffe captured the delicate white bloom of the jimsonweed, a common plant often found growing on waste land, zooming in to express every detail of the flower.

1934
Smooth sculptures
British artist Barbara Hepworth combined two separate pieces of carved, polished alabaster rock in this semiabstract sculpture. Rather than create a model to help her plan the piece, Hepworth carved directly into the stone, allowing her ideas to be shaped by the material. The simplified and streamlined shapes depict a reclining woman with a child on her knee.

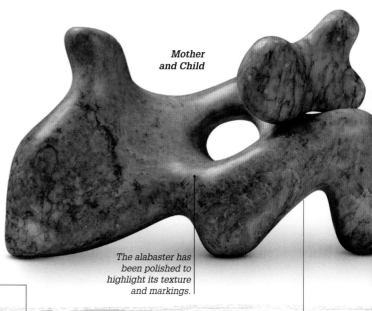

Mother and Child

The alabaster has been polished to highlight its texture and markings.

1930

Despite being simple, Mondrian's paintings took months to complete. He also never used a ruler to create the straight lines.

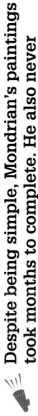

Composition with Red, Blue and Yellow

1930
Simplified art
Dutch artist Piet Mondrian became fascinated with reducing art to its most basic form. He moved away from mixing colors together and instead used blocks of primary colors and thick black lines, as seen in this painting. He called this style of abstract art Neoplasticism.

1934
Modern Indian art
Amrita Sher-Gil, one of India's most influential modern artists, is known for the use of bold colors in paintings that depicted the everyday lives of women. In *The Little Girl in Blue*, a young girl in vibrant turquoise stares off into space as though deep in thought.

The Little Girl in Blue

1924–1966   SURREALISM

Some early 20th century artists became interested in the recent developments in psychology, which suggested that dreams had special meanings. Surrealist art explored the relationship between dreams and reality, with the artists unlocking their imagination and taking inspiration from everyday items, often adding an element of surprise to their works.

Bizarre crustacean

Spanish artist Salvador Dali's *Lobster Telephone* (1936) is a classic example of a Surrealist object. The unexpected combination of the lobster and the phone is both funny and alarming— like something out of a strange dream.

The Terrace at Vernonnet

1939

Tapestry of colors

French painter Pierre Bonnard was fascinated by pattern. *The Terrace at Vernonnet* shows a group of people enjoying food and drink on a sunny terrace. Bonnard used intense patches of color to merge the figures and the garden together.

1935

1940 ▶▶

1936

Migrant mother

Photography was becoming a powerful way to tell news stories. American photojournalist Dorothea Lange took this picture of children clinging to their tired mother at a camp for migrant workers in California. It became a symbol of the hardship faced by so many during the Great Depression.

The use of simple shapes in the background shows the influence of Cubism.

1936

Life in Harlem

Documenting the years leading up to the Civil Rights Movement, American artist Norman Lewis produced paintings that focused on the lives and struggles of the Black community in Harlem in New York City. *Girl with Yellow Hat* is painted on coarse burlap fabric, creating texture that contrasts with the fine, neat clothes of the young woman, who sits alone, preoccupied in her own thoughts.

Girl with Yellow Hat

1940 ▶ 1960

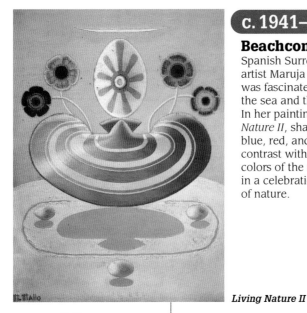
Living Nature II

Beachcombing

Spanish Surrealist artist Maruja Mallo was fascinated by the sea and the beach. In her painting *Living Nature II*, shades of blue, red, and pink contrast with the pale colors of the shells in a celebration of nature.

Office in a Small City

1953

Figures in isolation

American artist Edward Hopper was known for his realistic depictions of everyday urban scenes, often highlighting a sense of loneliness through solitary figures. *Office in a Small City* shows a man sitting in a corner office overlooking a concrete city while lost in a daydream.

1940

1950

1946

Folk hero

An outlaw who became a folk hero, Ned Kelly inspired a series of 27 paintings by Australian artist Sidney Nolan. In this work, the character is seen riding out across the desolate Australian outback in his trademark square helmet and armor.

Ned Kelly

Sidney Nolan's work was well-known for capturing the heat and emptiness of the vast Australian landscape.

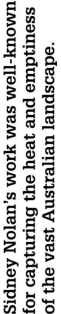

Self-portrait

c. 1950s

Through the lens

Seydou Keïta, one of Africa's most celebrated portrait photographers, documented the people of his home country Mali and the changing society of West Africa. In this rare self-portrait, he poses with a flower, looking directly into the camera.

Untitled

This sculpture is
made with brass
and steel wires.

1960

1953–1954

Woven sculpture

Influenced by
Mexican basket
weaving, Japanese-
American artist Ruth
Asawa created hanging
sculptures—some almost
6 ft (2 m) tall—using
interlocking looped wires.
The organic shapes resemble
human bodies or even
a mesh of spiders' webs.

> **"Art is
> doing. Art
> directly deals
> with life. "**
>
> Ruth Asawa,
> 1926–2013

1940–1960   ABSTRACT EXPRESSIONISM

In the 1940s, a group of mainly New York–based
American painters that included Jackson Pollock, Mark
Rothko, and Willem de Kooning began making art that
was abstract, but also expressed emotion through the use
of bold colors and brush strokes. This became known as
Abstract Expressionism. Their work can be divided into
two groups: "action painting" and "color field painting."

Action painting
Painted on the floor of Jackson Pollock's studio, *Blue Poles* (1952) was
created by pouring, flicking, and dripping household paint. This style is
an example of action painting. Pollock would dance around the canvas,
spontaneously and rhythmically applying layer upon layer of paint.

Color field painting
Mark Rothko was a pioneer of color field painting,
which focused on large blocks of color. In *White Center
(Yellow, Pink, and Lavender on Rose)* from 1950, the canvas
is divided into horizontal bands of color, which appear
to float over the orangey-red background.

The diving champion

Champion diver Helen Crlenkovich appears twice, diving gracefully over the skyline of modern-day San Francisco. Groups of people on both sides, some dressed in bathing suits themselves, look up at Crlenkovich as her body arches through the air.

Ancient and modern

At the center of the scene stands a tower, part stone and part machine, which symbolizes the coming together of ancient and modern life. It was inspired by the Aztec goddess Coatlicue and a machine Rivera had seen at a Ford Motors factory in the US.

Indigenous art

On the far left, Rivera celebrates Mexico's cultural history prior to its colonization by Spain. Indigenous artists carve, weave, and sculpt objects, while the Aztec feathered serpent god Quetzalcoatl coils around the scene.

Frida Kahlo

Mexican artist Frida Kahlo, who was also Rivera's wife, is depicted holding a paintbrush and palette. She is dressed in a traditional top and brightly colored skirt, representing her Mexican heritage.

Uniting cultures

Pan American Unity, 1940, Diego Rivera

This 73-ft- (22-m-) wide mural was created by Mexican artist Diego Rivera for an art fair in San Francisco. It tells the story of North America across its five panels, featuring everything from the Indigenous cultures of Mexico to the technological developments of the United States. Its detailed scenes contain many famous people, including some of Rivera's friends. By blending elements from the north and south of the continent, Rivera portrays his hope for a united future.

Technology
New farm machinery and the modern railroads represent the industrialization of the United States. The scene also celebrates the contribution of workers to the progress of society.

Unfinished plans
Rivera's friend, American architect Timothy Pflueger, stands holding plans for a building. It was Pflueger who invited Rivera to paint this mural for a library, which was unfortunately never built.

An inventor
American Samuel Morse, who invented the telegraph and Morse code, is seen holding a telegraph message tape. The globe in front of him, showing North and South America, is a reference to the brutal European colonization of the Americas.

1960 ▶ 1970

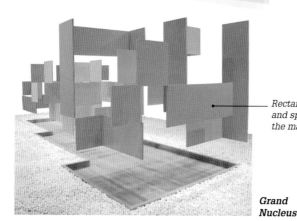

Grand
Nucleus

Rectangular panels
and spaces make up
the maze.

1965
Video art
Korean-American artist Nam June Paik is considered the founder of video art, basing his work around ordinary television sets. In a piece called *Magnet TV*, he used an industrial magnet to interfere with a television's signal, creating a rippling pattern across the screen.

Moving the magnet would change the image on the TV screen.

The shifting abstract patterns are a form of performance art.

Magnet TV

1960–1966
Walk-in artwork
Brazilian artist Hélio Oiticica wanted to challenge the way that art was experienced. He created 3D artwork called "habitable paintings" that viewers could walk around and explore. In *Grand Nucleus*, Oiticica built a futuristic maze made up of orange walls suspended in mid-air.

⏵⏵ 1960

1970

Hesitate

1964
Pueblo pottery
This characterful figure of an owl draws on the long tradition of pottery of the Indigenous Zuni people of New Mexico with its distinctive white markings on reddish clay. Owls symbolize patience and wisdom in Zuni art, and are also seen as protectors of the home.

Pottery owl
with a chick

1964
Seeing is believing
British artist Bridget Riley experimented with paintings that created optical illusions— a style known as op art (short for "optical art"). In her work *Hesitate*, carefully spaced monochrome circles and ovals appear to move before the eyes like a rolling wave.

1950–1960s POP ART

In the mid-20th century, the Pop Art movement took modern art in a different direction. Instead of taking inspiration from art in museums, American artists such as Andy Warhol, Jasper Johns, and Roy Lichtenstein turned to everyday objects and popular culture—including comic books, pop music, movies, and images from advertising. They broke down the barriers between what was considered "high art" and "low art" at the time, and made art more accessible for everyone.

Art from advertising

Inspired by advertising and images on TV, American artist Andy Warhol chose to turn everyday objects into art. He reproduced the outline of a soup can, as shown here in *Campbell's Soup Can (Tomato)* from 1962, and created a whole series called *Campbell's Soup Cans*. Warhol considered art to be a business, and wanted people to buy his paintings like they would buy soup cans from a grocery store.

Paint brushes

At first glance, this work by American artist Jasper Johns appears to be his paintbrushes in a coffee can, but it is in fact, a hand-painted bronze sculpture. Johns created *Bronze Brushes* in 1960 as part of a series exploring the boundary between painting and sculpture.

Comic book art

A scene from a comic book inspired American artist Roy Lichtenstein to paint *Whaam!* in 1963. This 13-ft- (4-m-) wide action-packed painting gets its title from the large bold lettering that represents the sound of a fighter jet being blown out of the sky by a missile. Lichtenstein used layers of different colored dots on top of each other to create shades of color. He even invented a special easel that could rotate, making it easier for him to paint the dots from different angles.

1970 ▸ 1980

Madhubani Bahir

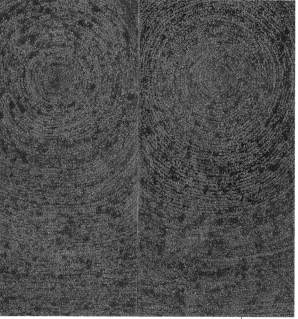

05-IV-71 #200 (Universe)

1971
Star-gazing
Kim Whanki led Korea's abstract art movement. His large swirling painting *05-IV-71 #200 (Universe)* represents the countless stars that make up the universe. The artist painted tiny white rectangles and filled them with blue dots, using a variety of blue tones to create depth. Kim wanted the spirals to soothe the eye while creating the effect of the cosmos stretching out to infinity.

1972
Colorful folk traditions
Madhubani Bahir is an example of a vibrant folk art style called Madhubani, which originated in Bihar, India. This painting by an unknown artist shows a pair of women on either side of a bright sun, surrounded by plants and flowers. Madhubani art is traditionally made by women, often using their fingers, sticks, and pen nibs. Originally painted on mud walls, they are now also made on fabric, canvas, and paper.

1970

 Valley Curtain stayed up for only 28 hours before it was taken down due to strong gale force winds.

Valley Curtain

1972
Covering the landscape
Bulgarian-born Christo and Moroccan-born Jeanne-Claude created art together, and were known for their large-scale outdoor installations, which included wrapping large buildings in fabric. *Valley Curtain* was a 1,250-ft- (381-m-) wide nylon fabric curtain that was hung across a state highway in Colorado. The artists chose a striking orange color to contrast with the surrounding countryside.

1977

Cloaked figures

British sculptor Lynn Chadwick is known for his large metal sculptures, which usually have humanlike bodies with geometric-shaped heads. In *Pair of Walking Figures—Jubilee*, Chadwick has created sculptures that appear to be moving, as their cloaks billow in the wind behind them.

Sinjerli Variation II

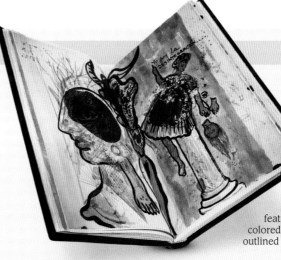

Pair of Walking Figures—Jubilee

1976

Minimalistic art

American artist Frank Stella was an innovator of Minimalism, a movement that saw artists move away from using real life as inspiration for their artwork, and instead focus on exploring shapes, colors, and materials. *Sinjerli Variation II* is a hand-knotted wool tapestry that shows interlocking bands of color.

1975   **1980**

DRAWING AND SKETCHING

Drawing is one of the oldest ways of expressing ideas in art. It is fundamental to all other art forms, with most artists drawing their ideas in pencil, charcoal, or ink before beginning their sculptures or paintings. Quickly made and loose drawings are called sketches.

Artist's sketchbook

Sketchbooks are a useful way for artists to note down their ideas, practice figures and motifs, and record their observations of the world around them. These pages from the sketchbook of Mexican artist Frida Kahlo feature drawings of women colored in vibrant ink and outlined with bold brushstrokes.

The sketch captures the essence of the original painting, but not the detail.

Studying the classics

Artists today, such as British-German painter Frank Auerbach, study and learn from the works of the great masters by sketching them. Auerbach was particularly captivated by Italian painter Titian's *Bacchus and Ariadne* (far left). His energetic sketch of the leaping Roman god Bacchus helped him create his own compositions when painting.

Day and night

Artists use a variety of techniques to convey light and dark, sunlight and moonlight, and the change from one to the other. Some represent brightness using simple patterns to show beams of light or halos. Others try to capture what they witness in nature, painting the colors, shadows, and atmospheric effects as they see and experience them.

Realistic sunset, 1643
French Baroque painter Claude Lorrain is well known for his closely observed, sunlit landscapes. In *Harbor Scene at Sunset*, he subtly grades the sky from blue to yellow to capture the glare of the setting sun, and highlights the tops of the waves caught by the dying light.

Daybreak, 1832
Dawn at Futamigaura by Utagawa Kunisada is a woodblock print from Japan's Edo period. It highlights the drama and grandeur of sunrise at a holy site. Sunbeams fan out like giant searchlights, making the onlookers by the rocks look tiny in comparison.

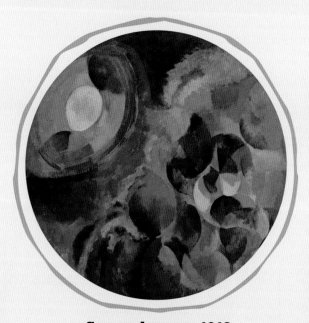

Sun and moon, 1913
Simultaneous Contrasts, by French abstract artist Robert Delaunay, represents the cycle of day and night: a rich explosion of color around the sun nudges into a moonlit sky. The circular shape represents the universe, and by blending and interweaving colors, Delaunay depicts the passing of time.

Dawn to dusk, 1892–1894
French Impressionist Claude Monet made 30 paintings of Rouen Cathedral, capturing the effects of light at different times of day. Around noon (left), the sun-drenched, peach-colored stone contrasts sharply with indigo shadows, but toward evening (right), the light and shadows blur into soft purples.

Hunting by torchlight, 1775

The Bhil people from central and western India are known for their hunting skills. This painting by an unknown artist shows four deer startled by the sudden glare of a hunter's torch. The torchlight is a stark contrast to the midnight-blue backdrop, and emphasizes the nighttime setting.

Moonlit winter, 1869

American artist Henry Farrer uses precise brushstrokes to apply cool blues and whites to *Winter Scene in Moonlight*, capturing the crisp chill of a moonlit winter landscape. With the ghostly silhouetted trees and light almost as bright as day, the scene appears both eerie and beautiful.

The startled deer stop in their tracks, making it easy to shoot them.

The cypress tree may represent a link between the Earth and Heaven.

Curved yellow brushstrokes circle the moon to create its "glow."

Heavenly stars, 1889

The Starry Night is one of Dutch artist Vincent Van Gogh's most recognizable paintings. Its swirling blue sky and blazing yellow-white stars are painted with great feeling, using thick, bold brushstrokes. It may reflect the artist's thoughts about nature, life, and death.

1980 ▶ 1990

STREET ART

The early street artists painted public areas with images as a form of protest. Street art can be controversial. Some people see it as vandalism and damage to public property, while others see it as a way to make art accessible to all.

Berlin Wall mural

Built in 1961, the Berlin Wall divided West and East Berlin in Germany during the Cold War. Artists began painting the Wall in 1984 and before long it was covered in images. This 2009 mural by Danish artist Birgit Kirke depicts a car crashing through the Wall. Its license plate shows the date the Wall fell in 1989.

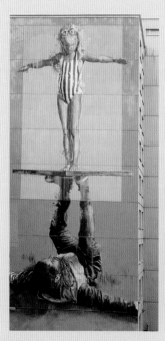

Street mural

Australian artist Fintan Magee's large-scale paintings often draw attention to isolated or abandoned buildings. Magee was invited to create this mural in 2017 for a street art festival in Finland. The towering mural, called *Balancing Act*, covers the wall of a multi-storey building, and depicts a young girl preparing to dive, supported from underneath by her father.

1980

1982
Street life

American artist Jean-Michel Basquiat started his career as a street graffiti artist in New York. His works were inspired by Black history and the difficulties he had faced in his own life. *Six Crimee* is a three-panel artwork that shows six Black figures with halos surrounded by chalked street games.

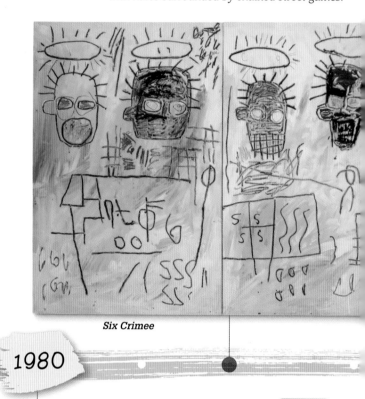

Six Crimee

1980
An unusual garden

French artist Niki de Saint Phalle created a magical world in the Tarot Garden in Tuscany, Italy. The sculpture park is made up of 22 fantastical giant figures, including this multi-colored bird named *The Sun*, which perches on an archway at the entrance.

The sculpture is covered with mosaics of mirrors, glass, and ceramic tiles.

The Sun

"It doesn't have to be pretty. It has to be meaningful."

Duane Hanson, 1925–1996

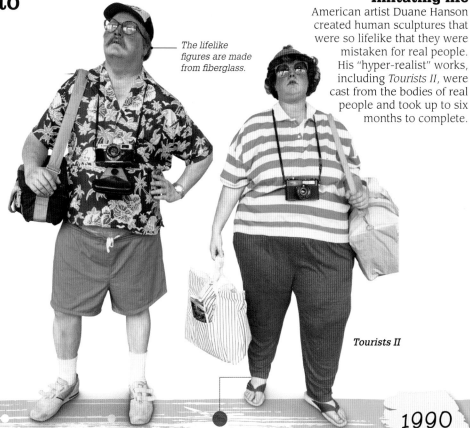

The lifelike figures are made from fiberglass.

Imitating life

American artist Duane Hanson created human sculptures that were so lifelike that they were mistaken for real people. His "hyper-realist" works, including *Tourists II*, were cast from the bodies of real people and took up to six months to complete.

Tourists II

1990 ▶▶

In a Hotel Bedroom

1985–1986

Painting beyond the frame

Instead of showing things in a realistic way, British artist Howard Hodgkin tried to capture his memory of events and places. *In a Hotel Bedroom* was painted on wood using brightly colored daubs of oil paint, which continue from the central picture out onto the frame.

1931–1998   HENRY MUNYARADZI

Zimbabwean sculptor Henry Munyaradzi was a leading member of the modern African sculpture movement known as Shona, which was inspired by the carvings of the Shona people of southern Africa. Munyaradzi retained the original shapes of the stones he used, sculpting simple forms inspired by the natural world and his spirituality.

Stone carvings

Carved from soapstone, *Spirit Protecting Orphans* (1996–1998) is a double-sided sculpture with a large face on one side and smaller figures on the other.

1990 ▶ 2000

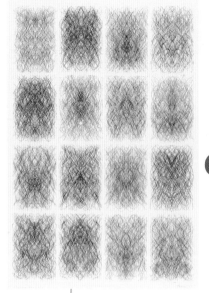

Visions of Hildegarde, M

1993
Telling stories
Portuguese-British artist Paula Rego enjoys creating stories in her paintings. In this work, she depicts a sculptor lost in thought, smoking a pipe in her studio, while her assistant paints a still life of cabbages. Rego has made the artist larger and more colorful than everything else.

1990
Digital art
American artist Roman Verostko was a pioneer of "algorithmic art"— art made from computer coding. Verostko designed his own software to plot the shapes he wanted to create. For *Visions of Hildegarde, M*, ink pens held by mechanical devices that followed his coding made the brightly colored lines.

1990 ▶▶ ⸻ **1995**

1991
Exploding onto the scene
British artist Cornelia Parker is known for installations that affect how we look at everyday objects. This one is created from the pieces of an exploded garden shed. Fragments are hung from the ceiling as if captured mid-explosion, and cast dark, dramatic shadows.

Cold Dark Matter: An Exploded View

1994
Everyday high art
Inspired by the readymades of Marcel Duchamp (see p.155), American artist Jeff Koons uses everyday objects in a humorous way. His *Balloon Dog* transforms a familiar childhood party object into a large, shiny "high art" sculpture. This work is part of a series that reinvents childhood possessions, including toys and lumps of modeling clay.

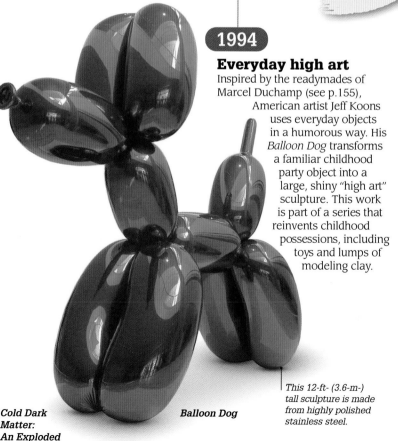

Balloon Dog

This 12-ft- (3.6-m-) tall sculpture is made from highly polished stainless steel.

1997
Vibrant memories

Self-taught Algerian artist Baya Mahieddine explores childhood memories and traditional African motifs in her paintings. In the watercolor and gouache *Two Women with Vase on a Yellow Background*, two women in flowery dresses are surrounded by fish and fruit. The painting is influenced by colorful African textiles and the repeating patterns in Islamic Art.

Two Women with Vase on a Yellow Background

1910–1996   EMILY KAME KNGWARREYE

First Nations Australian artist Emily Kame Kngwarreye only discovered painting in her late 70s, but painted more than 3,000 canvases in the eight years before her death.

She worked freely by layering lines and dots to create abstract compositions. Kngwarreye's work often explores First Nations stories of creation and tales about ancestral spirits, known as the Dreaming.

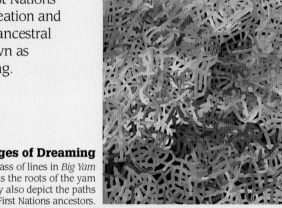

Images of Dreaming
The swirling mass of lines in *Big Yam* (1996) represents the roots of the yam plant, and may also depict the paths trodden by First Nations ancestors.

2000

1999
Mighty mother

At more than 30 ft (9 m) tall, this monumental steel spider looks frightening, but *Mother* actually depicts a protective parent figure. French-American artist Louise Bourgeois chose this creature because she was inspired by her mother's skill as a weaver.

Mother

Which side?

A white picket fence represents ideal middle-class life in the suburbs. By marking the gate as "Private" the artist signals that this is a deeply divided society. The viewer is left to wonder if the Black woman has been allowed into a place of privilege or if she is being excluded from another.

Pool rail

Three handrails jut out of the pool. The word "swan" on this one refers to a graceful, uncomplicated dive. Marshall used different dive positions on the rails to suggest the different ways people address Black history—some may dive in headfirst while others take a more complex way in.

Ocean-faring ship

A brightly colored toy boat moves across the pool, creating ripples in the water. But the pool is labeled "Atlantic Ocean," suggesting that the boat is not a toy, but represents a slave ship transporting African people to the Americas.

Painting Black history

Plunge, 1992, Kerry James Marshall

Black American artist Kerry James Marshall depicts the mistreatment and exclusion faced by Black people in bold and colorful paintings filled with symbolism. In *Plunge*, Marshall explores the history of the Middle Passage—the transportation of enslaved African people across the Atlantic Ocean to the Americas—by setting it in a backyard swimming pool in the suburbs.

Black bather

The woman standing at the edge of the diving board looks about to jump in, but her interlocked arms suggest she is nervous or unsure. The artist has used the figure's uncertainty to comment on how some people approach their past. Marshall is known for painting his figures using only black paint, in order to emphasize their Black identity.

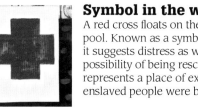

Symbol in the water

A red cross floats on the edge of the pool. Known as a symbol of protection, it suggests distress as well as the possibility of being rescued. It also represents a place of exchange, where enslaved people were bought or sold.

2000 ▶ 2020

2002

Reaching for hope

Girl with Balloon is a spray-painted mural by British street artist Banksy. Much reproduced, the original version was accompanied by the words "There is always hope." But is the girl grasping for the balloon or letting go of it? We do not know.

Girl with Balloon

The weather project, 2003

2003

Artificial sun

In *The weather project, 2003*, Icelandic-Danish artist Olafur Eliasson created the illusion of a giant sun by reflecting a semicircle of light from a vast mirrored ceiling. Visitors stretched out on the floor to bask in its glow.

2000

2010

2010

Seeing spots

This 10-ft- (3-m-) tall flower sculpture, part of a series, combines two constant themes in Japanese artist Yayoi Kusama's work: a passion for the natural world and an obsession with polka dots. For her, the dots represent the infinity of the universe, of which Earth—and all of us—are only a tiny part.

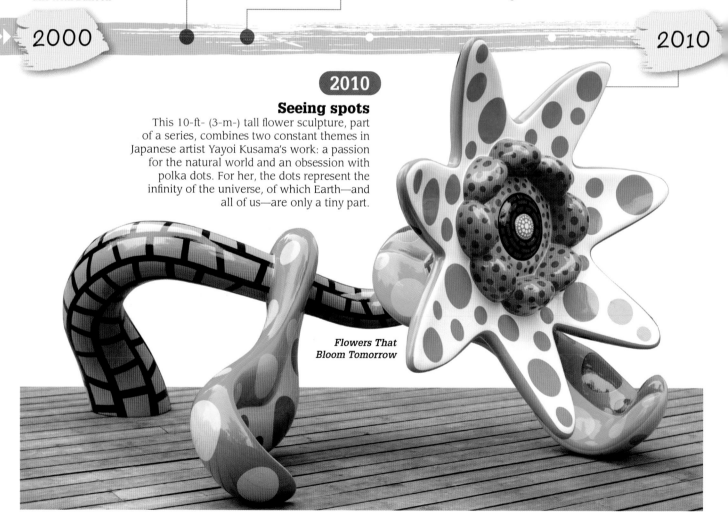

Flowers That Bloom Tomorrow

PUBLIC ART

Designed to be accessible to everyone for free, public art helps bring public spaces to life and gives people a sense of pride in their communities. Artworks may be temporary or permanent, and can take many forms—from sculptures and statues to performances. The best-loved examples are often interactive.

Cloud Gate, 2004
Created for a public park in Chicago, British-Indian artist Anish Kapoor's bean-shaped mirror reflects and distorts the city's skyline. Visitors can walk through its 12-ft- (3.7-m-) high archway.

The globe head represents cultural exchange between different nations.

Apollo of the Belvedere (After Leochares)

2017
Strike a pose
This work by British-Nigerian artist Yinka Shonibare reimagines a Classical sculpture of the Greek god Apollo. By incorporating African batik fabric into a sculpture that has its roots in Western art, he explores the issues of race, identity, and colonialism.

2020

2015
Capturing a memory
This piece by Peruvian artist Sandra Gamarra looks at first glance like a collage made up of picture fragments, but is in fact a delicately composed oil painting. She presents a series of Peruvian landscapes and jumbles them up in order to explore the process of how we remember what we see.

Re-creation of *Portrait of a Young Woman*

2020
Art in lockdown
With museums and galleries closed during the COVID-19 pandemic, art enthusiasts began creating their favorite artwork at home. American photographer Bryan Beasley re-created a 17th-century portrait by Dutch artist Nicolaes Pickenoy by asking his wife to pose with a paper fan, tinsel cuffs, and a DIY toilet roll collar.

The Frame Landscape II

181

Three Architects

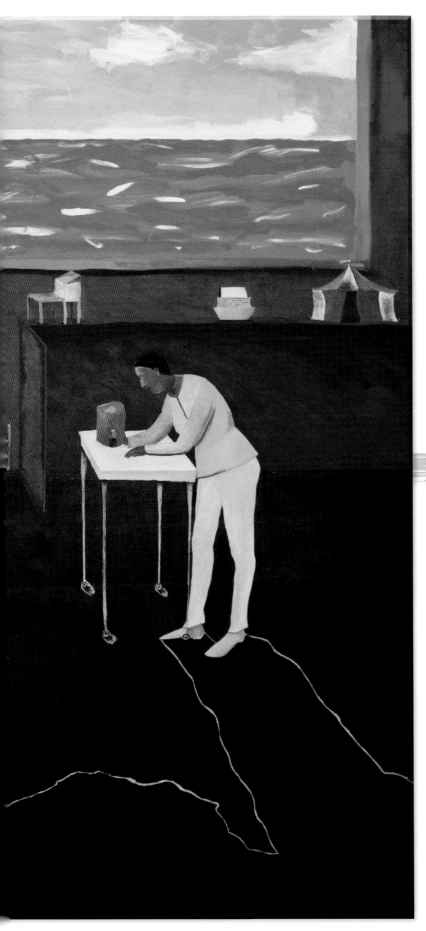

What happens next?

Born in Zanzibar, British artist Lubaina Himid is known for her vibrant paintings that celebrate the lives and experiences of Black people. Many of Himid's works are also a commentary on the absence of Black people in art, especially in scenes of everyday life. *Three Architects* shows three brightly dressed Black women in a design studio. Two of the women are discussing a model, while another woman is working alone behind them. Himid's art is inspired by theater design. This painting is like a scene in a play, inviting the viewer to step onto the stage to explore the stories that are unfolding, as well as questioning what might happen next.

Through two of her favorite themes, clothes and buildings, Himid tries to show that things are often designed without considering **the needs of women**.

Glossary

Terms defined elsewhere in the glossary are in *italics*.

abstract art
An artistic style that uses shapes, forms, marks, and colors to represent ideas or emotions, rather than showing them in a recognizable way.

Art Deco
An art style from the 1920s and 1930s with geometric patterns and streamlined shapes.

Art Nouveau
An art style beginning in the 1890s with flowing lines and stylized curved *motifs* inspired by plants.

artisan
A person who creates art and handicrafts for a living, often by hand.

Baroque
A grand, theatrical style of art and architecture popular in 17th-century Europe and Latin America.

bust
A sculpture of the upper body of a person.

Byzantine
Related to the ancient city of Byzantium (modern-day Istanbul) or the Eastern Roman Empire.

calligraphy
Decorative or ornamental writing.

ceramics
Objects such as pots, figures, or tiles made of clay.

chiaroscuro
A strong, dramatic contrast between light and shade in a painting.

Classical
Referring to the art, architecture, and cultural ideas of ancient Greece and Rome.

collage
A picture made by sticking pieces of paper, fabric, or other objects onto a surface.

Cubism
An art style from early 20th-century Europe showing objects or people from many different viewpoints at the same time, breaking them up into odd angles and fragments. It was created by the artists Pablo Picasso and Georges Braque.

diptych
A painting that consists of two panels or parts.

embroidery
The art of decorating fabric with stitched designs in wool or thread.

enamel
A glassy substance—opaque or transparent—that can be added to a hard surface to decorate or protect it.

engraving
A printing technique where cuts are made into a metal plate to capture ink and form a printed image. See also *print*.

Expressionism
An art style that was about feelings and emotions, often shown through distorted shapes or colors.

Fauvism
An early 20th-century movement, in which artists used simplified shapes, bold brushstrokes, and vibrant color to express a sense of wild, energetic emotion.

figurine
A small sculpted figure.

folk art
Traditional art made by hand for use by the craftsperson or a group of people.

foreshortening
A painting technique that shows a person or object in a way that gives the illusion of lengthening or projecting into a space.

fresco
A technique of painting, usually on a wall, using a mixture of powdered pigments and water on wet plaster.

frieze
A sculpted or decorated ornamental band on a building or piece of furniture.

gilded
To be covered with gold.

glaze
A thin, transparent coating on a surface that protects it, makes it waterproof, and can add decoration. A glaze is also the name given to a layer of *oil paint*.

Gothic
A western European style of architecture, painting, and sculpture that flourished between the 12th and 15th centuries.

gouache
A water-soluble paint that is opaque, so the white surface of the paper does not show through.

Hudson River School
The name given to a group of 19th-century American artists, starting in the Hudson River Valley in New York, who painted landscapes, capturing the natural beauty of the country.

hyper-realism
An art style from the early 1970s, in which artists created enhanced sculptures and paintings showing scenes from everyday life, making art more vivid than a photograph.

icon
In painting, this term refers to an image of Jesus Christ, the Virgin Mary, a saint, or another holy person.

illuminated manuscript
A book or paper that has been decorated with richly colored drawings and occasionally silver or gold.

Impressionism
An art style that focused on color and the changing effects of light. Impressionist artists often painted outdoors and tried to capture passing moments.

installation
A work of art, often mixed media and of several pieces, that is exhibited in a large space.

lacquer
A hard coating added to an object to protect it and provide decoration.

landscape
A scene or painting of a scene, usually in the countryside.

Mannerism
An art style that developed between 1520 and 1600 showing people in exaggerated forms, odd settings, and unnatural colors.

manuscript
A book or document that is written and sometimes decorated by hand.

miniature
A small painting, often a *portrait*.

Minimalism
A form of *abstract art* from the United States in the 1960s using simple geometric shapes based on squares and rectangles.

Modernism
A broad term for describing beliefs, attitudes, art, and architecture from the late 19th century to the mid-20th century.

monochrome
An object or painting that has only one color.

mosaic
A picture made up of small pieces, usually tiles made of glass, clay, or stone.

motif
A repeated or recurring theme or pattern in a work of art.

mural
A picture painted directly onto a wall.

Neoclassicism
A style inspired by ancient Greek and Roman art and architecture. It became popular in the late 18th and 19th centuries.

netsuke
A traditional Japanese fastening, often carved into animal shapes, used with a cord to hang a pouch from a sash.

oil paint
A slow-drying paint made by mixing *pigments* with an oil.

perspective
The art of creating depth or distance in a painting, in order to make objects and people appear three-dimensional.

photojournalism
A style of journalism that communicates a news story using photography.

pigment
A colored powder that is mixed with a binder—such as gum, oil, or acrylic—to make paints.

Pointillism
A painting technique developed by Georges Seurat, using dots of complementary colors. Viewed at a distance, the eye blends the dots together to create areas of solid color.

Pop Art
An art style beginning in the mid-1900s that was inspired by and mimicked popular culture.

porcelain
A white, clay-based material that is used to make china (or *ceramics*).

portrait
Painting, sculpture, or other art that shows an image of a person or a group of people.

Post-Impressionism
The term used to describe an art style that followed *Impressionism*, responding to the style, taking it further, and sometimes challenging its ideals.

Pre-Raphaelites
A group of 19th-century British painters. They were against the promotion by London's Royal Academy of *Renaissance* painter Raphael as an ideal artist.

print
A way of transferring an image from one surface to another. Prints are often made by spreading ink over a raised or engraved design and pressing it onto paper. See also *engraving*.

proportion
Refers to how the sizes of different elements in a work of art relate to each other—for example, the size of someone's head in relation to their body.

readymades
A name given by the artist Marcel Duchamp to works consisting of ordinary, manufactured objects that are presented as art.

Realism
An art style that began in the 1850s, which showed modern life in a realistic way using ordinary people and everyday objects.

relic
An object made holy because of its association with a saint or martyr.

relief
A *sculpture* on a wall—elements stand out from a flat base against the wall.

Renaissance
A cultural movement that began in Italy in the 14th century, inspired by the artistic ideals of ancient Greece and Rome.

Romanesque
A style of art and architecture that developed in 10th-century Germany, and later spread throughout Europe. The style was likened to that of ancient Roman architecture.

Romantic
A painter or painting of the 19th-century movement Romanticism, in which artists painted in a dramatic, emotional style, often showing a person surrounded by a wild and stormy *landscape*.

sculpture
Art created by carving, shaping, or molding materials such as marble, clay, or wood into abstract or realistic figures.

semi-abstract
A piece of art where the subject is recognizable although the forms are styled from *abstract art*.

sfumato
A method of gradually blending colors in a painting to create blurred, soft outlines. It was created by the artist Leonardo da Vinci.

sketch
A rough drawing or painting, often made to help plan a final artwork.

statuette
A small statue.

still life
An arrangement of objects, such as flowers or fruit, set up for an artist to paint or photograph.

Surrealism
An art style beginning around the 1920s that expressed thoughts of the unconscious mind through startling and confusing dreamlike paintings and objects.

symbolism
Using symbols to represent ideas and emotions.

terra-cotta
Baked or fired clay, usually reddish-brown in color.

textile
A woven or knitted cloth.

triptych
A painting that consists of three panels or parts.

ukiyo-e
Meaning "pictures of the floating world," this Japanese *woodblock print* and painting style from the 17th to the 19th centuries showed scenes from history and folk tales, as well as daily life.

watercolor
A water-based paint with a light, transparent color quality; also a painting made with these paints.

woodblock printing
To carve an image out of a block of wood, which is then inked and placed against paper, usually in a press, to make a *print*.

▶▶Index

Acknowledgments

Dorling Kindersley would like to thank the following people for their help with making the book: Edward Aves, Bipasha Roy, Kelsie Besaw, Arpit Aggarwal, Sreshtha Bhattacharya, Hina Jain, Virien Chopra, Rupa Rao, and Carron Brown for editorial assistance; Mohammad Rizwan and Jagtar Singh for DTP assistance; Suhita Dharamjit and Saloni Singh for the jacket; Dr. Vivian Delgado, Joy Onyejiako, Dr. Caroline Dodds Pennock, and Shelley Ware for authenticity checks; Hazel Beynon for proofreading; and Carron Brown for the index.

Smithsonian Enterprises:
Kealy Gordon, Product Development Manager
Jill Corcoran, Director, Licensed Publishing
Brigid Ferraro, Vice President, Business Development
 and Licensing
Carol LeBlanc, President.

The publisher would like to thank the following for their kind permission to reproduce their photographs:
(Key: a-above; b-below/bottom; c-center; f-far; l-left; r-right; t-top)